Mindfulness and Meditation

Step Approach to Reduce Stress, Anxiety and Enjoy Your Life Now

(Ensure a Deep Sleep With Guided Meditation)

Marco Loflin

Published by Rob Miles

© **Marco Loflin**

All Rights Reserved

Mindfulness and Meditation: Step Approach to Reduce Stress, Anxiety and Enjoy Your Life Now (Ensure a Deep Sleep With Guided Meditation)

ISBN 978-1-989990-98-8

All rights reserved. No part of this guide may be reproduced in any form without permission in writing from the publisher except in the case of brief quotations embodied in critical articles or reviews.

Legal & Disclaimer

The information contained in this book is not designed to replace or take the place of any form of medicine or professional medical advice. The information in this book has been provided for educational and entertainment purposes only.

The information contained in this book has been compiled from sources deemed reliable, and it is accurate to the best of the Author's knowledge; however, the Author cannot guarantee its accuracy and validity and cannot be held liable for any errors or omissions. Changes are periodically made to this book. You must consult your doctor or get professional medical advice before using any of the suggested remedies, techniques, or information in this book.

Upon using the information contained in this book, you agree to hold harmless the Author from and against any damages, costs, and expenses, including any legal fees potentially resulting from the application of any of the information provided by this guide. This disclaimer applies to any damages or injury caused by the use and application, whether directly or indirectly, of any advice or information presented, whether for breach of contract, tort, negligence, personal injury, criminal intent, or under any other cause of action.

You agree to accept all risks of using the information presented inside this book. You need to consult a professional medical practitioner in order to ensure you are both able and healthy enough to participate in this program.

Table of Contents

INTRODUCTION 1

CHAPTER 1: IS MEDITATION SAFE? 4

CHAPTER 2: GUIDED MINDFULNESS MEDITATIONS 13

CHAPTER 3: WHAT IS MINDFULNESS? 21

CHAPTER 4: WHAT IS MEDITATION? 27

CHAPTER 5: THE POWER OF LOOKING INWARD 35

CHAPTER 6: THE 'WHY' OF MINDFULNESS 46

CHAPTER 7: ORIGIN OF MINDFULNESS 51

CHAPTER 8: WHAT IS MEDITATION? 56

CHAPTER 9: WHY MEDITATION IS GOOD FOR YOU? 60

CHAPTER 10: 12 INDISPENSABLE MINDFUL LIVING TOOLS 64

CHAPTER 11: APPLYING THESE TECHNIQUES TO EVERYDAY SITUATIONS 74

CHAPTER 12: MINDFULNESS 78

CHAPTER 13: SO WHAT IS THIS MINDFULNESS ALL ABOUT? 82

CHAPTER 14: WHY MINDFULNESS IS A GOOD PLACE TO START 88

CHAPTER 15: WHAT IS MEDITATION? 94

CHAPTER 16: WHY WE ARE UNHAPPY: WE ARE UNHAPPY BECAUSE WE ARE FORGETFUL 100

CHAPTER 17: EARLY ENCOUNTER WITH MEDITATION ... 106

CHAPTER 18: WHAT IS MINDFULNESS? 110

CHAPTER 19: STRESS MANAGEMENT 120

CHAPTER 20: DEALING WITH NEGATIVE THOUGHTS 137

CHAPTER 21: TIPS ABOUT MINDFULNESS EXERCISES 148

CHAPTER 22: ACCEPTING WHERE YOU ARE TO GET WHERE YOU WANT TO BE 164

CONCLUSION 181

Introduction

A lot of us go through life every day as a constant cycle of the same thing in and out, day after day—waking up, eating, going to work, coming home and watching the television then going to bed. This is leaving people feeling unfulfilled, bored, wanting to do things that are extravagant to give them excitement in their lives and ultimately, the planet is then left with miserable people living miserable mundane lives. Fortunately, this is all beginning to change.

People around us are waking up, they are becoming mindful of what the world really is, what they really are and mainly, what inner power they hold within themselves. We are all infinite creators, we are infinite beings, that carry the Universe within us. When we connect to this inner being that we all carry our world begins to look different around us. We awaken to our potential and our infinite powers, we start to connect with our consciousness and start living the type of life we have always desired.

What are the benefits of the learning this?

If we really want to break free of routine, unfulfillment, and sameness, we have to breach the borders of the realms we see before us. No longer can we look at the world through materialistic eyes. We must instead, expand our vision and look at it through the eyes of our souls because it is when we do that, that we begin to see real changes.

We are not supposed to be going to jobs we dislike to try to make money. We should be making plenty of money by doing the jobs we love. We are not supposed to be filling our bodies with toxins and poisons labeled 'food.' We are supposed to fill our bodies with pure high vibrational foods that awaken us and make us feel alive. We are not supposed to be watching our children grow up in front of TV screen that shows violence and put pressure on them to learn things that do not give them joy. We are supposed to love them, show them how to be kind and loving, all the while teaching them the importance of loving their own selves so that they can have a truly blessed life.

The world is a little backward at the moment but more and more people are beginning to wake up all around the world and this book will give you some of the tools to learn how to awaken yourself.

Chapter 1: Is Meditation Safe?

I'm not aware of any person that has been hurt because they were meditating.

There have been some concerns raised about some breathing exercises used by some meditators. I don't use any other than the simple, guided breath routine which I explain later.

As with any change in your lifestyle or exercise pattern, I recommend that you discuss your intention to do some meditation with your medical advisor.

They can relate the activity to their deep knowledge of your personal medical history, needs and current condition. Please follow their advice.

Meditation is the subject of ongoing research in several countries. One study which I mention in the book reviewed over 100 quality research projects and found positive, measurable benefits for people with anxiety or depression.

But, each person's situation and needs is different so please do your own checking as well.

Who Controls Your Mind?

The modern lifestyle makes great demands on us and there are plenty of people who try to control how we live and what we think.

When we turn to TV or other media, we are confronted by a lot of negativity and sensation. This can make us fearful and uncertain about our future or even our present situation.

We are offered many ways to escape from our worries while they suggest that we cannot cope without their help and products they recommend.

A lot of these negative influences flow into our minds without conscious effort on our part to review or even understand them. They're part of the

background noise which we have got used to listening to while we work or try to relax doing other things. But, there is a significant influence from the media on our subconscious mind. It absorbs what we hear as fact. Over time, these messages affect how our physical and mental systems operate, develop and react to situations we get into.

Over time, the doubts and fears that were implanted have more control over our confidence and competence.

The way our communities are developing means that many people have become more isolated. People often don't know their neighbors at all. This means the negativity which flows into our minds has greater effect on some.

Depression and anxiety are rampant through our cities and even smaller communities as well.

Mindfulness meditation can help to bring your thoughts back under your control as you become more aware of the abilities you have and how you can use them better.

This has helped many people reduce the amount of worry they suffer from and get enjoyment from their daily activities. It would be worth the time and effort needed to get started just for that. wouldn't it?

But, over time, using any form of meditation will help you improve your self-confidence and be better able to get along with other people. I just think that the mindfulness form is easier to try for people who have limited time and no background of meditation. A few sessions have little effect, so don't worry. You probably need more time. Remember that the cost of these sessions is almost zero, the potential benefits can improve every day for the rest of your life! You are not just taking back control of your thoughts, you are gaining a better focus which will improve your social and business relationships.

Benefits of Meditation

The benefits of meditation which I mention here are some which can be achieved with any form of meditation. There are quality studies of the effects of meditation on people that have symptoms of depressions which are very encouraging.

From experience and research, I believe

that meditation can help many people by:
Improving our ability to focus more keenly without extra effort on the most important aspects of our work and private life.

Removing the affects of useless emotional baggage which has a negative hold on so many people.

Allowing us to develop a better understanding of our needs and abilities.

Developing more control over our thoughts so we can eliminate the negative influences and deal rationally with problems as they arise.

Becoming more confident about our current skills and our ability to improve them or learn new ones because we are able to focus and learn more efficiently.

Being more attentive to everyone we deal with which will promote a noticeable improvement in our business dealings and relationships.

Giving us greater understanding of other people because we removed much of our emotional biases.

The benefits are not all achieved to a high level by everyone that does meditation, of course.

But, most people will see some measurable benefit from the practice in their own well-being and their interactions with other people in all areas of their life.

That leaves two questions which must be considered before starting to invest time and other resources in meditation. I have addressed the question of how safe meditation is in a separate chapter. So, look at what you must invest to get the benefits.
The biggest cost is your time.

I'd estimate that you could expect to get some good effect from using meditation techniques if you did three or four 30-minute sessions a week for six months.

That's two hours a week and about 48 hours in all.

It's for you to judge if that is worthwhile. Remember that there are few other costs involved unless you join a formal program, buy special clothing and a mat etc.

Most of us can find two hours a week when it does not have to be at the same time or on the same days each week. The important factor is to do the sessions every week.

Could you make better progress by investing more time over a shorter period? That's possible but it depends on your own personality and how much practice you can accept to maintain your enthusiasm.

If you slowly increase the number of sessions each week, you may find some point where you feel you are doing enough and to do any more each week would interfere with other important things in your life.

The stronger self-confidence we develop through meditation will also help us to set and achieve higher personal and professional goals for the rest of our lives.

There is no limit on when you can start meditation or most other projects which might appeal to you.

But, I hope that you will agree after reading this book and trying some of the strategies and tips, the sooner you start, the more benefits you can look forward to!

You will find that your greater confidence from your meditation and dealing with your negative mental thoughts and emotions will help you be more successful in other areas like making and keeping to a better diet and exercise program.

This opens the door to making larger goals and having greater confidence that you can achieve them. It depends what you want from life. When you have achieved some success which has previously eluded you, you will really understand that he sky is no longer the limit for you!

Chapter 2: Guided Mindfulness Meditations

Here are some exercises to get your started:

For Self-Acceptance

Settle into your mediation area. You can play some "meditation" songs if you want.

Allow yourself to be come into that peaceful state where you can open up your mind and your body.

Quiet the body, relax, and focus on that wall or object in front of you.

Then pay attention to your body.

Feel the sensations – do not just think about the sensations moving into your body as you breathe, feel them as they move directly into your body.

Feel the pull of gravity. Feel the sensations. Feel the awareness and sensations meeting from moment to moment.

Feel the sensations in your chest as you continue with your rhythmic breathing. Feel you muscles expanding and contracting.

Be aware of how your breath envelops your whole body.

Go to that place within you where you feel most safe and secured, loved and adored, where it feels good to be appreciated and recognized.

As you allow your body to breathe and become alive, feel that place and realize that your life is sacred.

Say to yourself:

"I open my heart to all the parts of myself – I recognize the infant, the child, the teenager, the young adult, the adult, my present, and my future self – I accept them. I recognize them all.

I fully accept that every embarrassment, mistake, and every hurt I experienced, are all part of my story. And my story includes every success, every triumph, every mistake, and every failure.

All of these are valuable. I may not completely understand how but I accept them all.

Right in this moment, I choose to love every part of myself. I choose to accept all the strengths and the weaknesses, the beautiful and the not so beautiful, and the good and the bad.

I have true compassion for myself. I feel compassion for others.

I create a life of acceptance, understanding, and compassion.

I choose love. I choose acceptance.

I radiate acceptance.

I accept myself.

I radiate acceptance.

And so it is. I'll stay in this wonderful and serene place for love, understanding, and acceptance for as long as I can."

"Return" to the room slowly and gently.

As you end the meditation session, feel rejuvenated. Feel how alive you are.

Feel the love and acceptance in your heart.

Continue to radiate positive vibes.

For Self-Confidence

Settle into your space and play some meditation music.

This is an exercise to help boost your self-confidence and remind yourself that all you need is to find time to relax to find your confidence again.

Take time for your body and your mind, especially for your soul.

Forget the worries of everyday life and just allow your mind and your body that much needed break from thoughts that can be tiring.

Enter into a world where you are the center of everything, where you have total control of your mind and your body.

Now begin to breathe in and imagine that the air entering your mouth down to your body is pure and clean. Hold your breath for a few seconds and feel your body begin to relax.

Now you can exhale.

Breathe in again and then breathe out.

The air you breathe out is hot. It is full of tensions that cause you to be anxious and worried.

Focus on your breathing — every single moment that you breathe, feel it. Feel the air coming in and out of your mouth.

As you breathe out, feel the tensions leaving from your body.

Focus on your breathing. Feel every single moment.

Let the tensions out of your body.

Allow your mind to slow down. As you continue breathing in and breathing out, allow your body to stop and just relax.

Keep breathing.

Each time you inhale, feel the warm sensations of fresh air filling your whole body – relaxing it.

Feel the air. That air is pure and free from all of your anxieties.

Continue to breathe in and breathe in.

By now, your breathing becomes deeper. It is starting to get more intense but at the same time, your breathing is leading your body to an ultimate relaxation state.

Your mind will slowly begin to have thoughts that are beyond your control, do not worry about because it is normal. This allows your mind to release negative sensations, negative thoughts, and bad feelings.

As you continue to go deeper into your meditative state, these negative thoughts will gradually quiet down.

Then you continue to experience deep relaxation.

You will feel your body entering into a sense of peace.

You will the mind getting lighter as you reach the calm and peace you deserve.

You begin to feel light.

Be aware of the music that feels the entire room. Feel the sensations running down deep inside your body, then to your soul, and then to your spirit.

Breathe in. Breathe out.

You are slowly entering a universe of peace, serenity, and harmony.

Breathe in. Breathe out.

As you calm your breathing, you also calm your mind.

Repeat these words to yourself:

"I am light. I am release negativity. I release negativity. I am confident. I can do anything. I can achieve anything. I am light."

Breathe in. Breathe out.

Feel your breathing.

You can alternatively use these words:

"I am now relaxed. I am calm. I deserve this. I deserve to be in this calm and peaceful universe. I am becoming more relaxed. I am more relaxed. I am more confident."

Take a deep breath and release.

Breathe again, inhale, and exhale, while being aware of every tension that you are feeling.

You feel relaxed now.

You feel more relaxed.

You feel more confident now.

Stay still and enjoy the moment.

You can practice this anytime you are feeling frustrated and stressed because of the challenges of everyday life.

When you feel challenged, stop for a while and breathe. Calm your body so you can calm your mind.

Breathe in. Breathe out. Relax. Feel confident.

Chapter 3: What Is Mindfulness?

The thing with the idea of mindfulness that people argue about is that when you relax, you put everything out of your mind. How can you then be mindful? Isn't the idea to drop thoughts and think of nothing? When you are first introduced to mindfulness, you have just have a teacher who asks you to do just that and think of nothing for a moment, to show you how preposterous that is for someone coming to a class in order to find a way to relax. The last thing your mind wants is emptiness. It's not accustomed to it and it doesn't know how to handle silence.

Try it for a moment. Sit in a comfortable position and try to think of nothing and time yourself. The chances are it won't be long before thoughts start to creep into your head and you are back to square one again. The fact is that ever since you were a child, you have been encouraged to think:

Think before you speak, child.

I can still hear the voice of my mother using this phrase when I was perhaps a little unkind to my siblings. However, mindfulness isn't about letting go of all thought. It's about opening up your senses. It's also about disciplining your mind in a certain manner so that it doesn't give you all the random thoughts that you are having trouble coping with. How does one do that? Well, that's where mindfulness comes in and one of the first lessons that you are taught is that there is a certain way to breathe so that you are able to give your body the amount of oxygen that it requires. You may not know it, but the average human being only uses about a third of their lung capacity. When you learn to breathe deeply during your mindfulness lesson, you will find that this improves a lot of things inside you. Your sympathetic nervous system is permitted to spread the oxygen to all of the parts of your body that need it and that's quite a lot. Did you know that this controls the temperature of the body? It also helps the digestive system and above all else, it means that you have the right amount of oxygen circulating in your blood. When you over-oxygenate, that's when panic sets in, so it's fairly obvious that the breathing method that you employ makes you calmer.

The second thing you will learn is how you control the thoughts that go through your head. When you think of the past, for example, you are wasting the moment because you are not really in it. The past has gone and there is very little that you can do to change it, so why waste the energy? The same thing happens when you worry about the future. You waste the energy you should be putting into this moment on things that have not yet happened. There's a very good demonstration of what the Dalai Lama said when he was asked about what amazed him most about mankind. It was mankind itself and this is the phrase that he came up with that may help you to understand a little more about mindfulness.

"Man surprised me most about humanity. Because he sacrifices his health in order to make money. Then he sacrifices money to recuperate his health. And then he is so anxious about the future that he does not enjoy the present; the result being that he does not live in the present or the future. He lives as if he is never going to die and then dies, having never really lived."

It is a very astute quotation because it relates to the way in which people choose to live their lives and so much time is passing by without actually enjoying the moment. Mindfulness takes you back to this moment so that you start to enjoy life more and can feel, hear, taste and enjoy every nuance that this moment offers you. Thereby, you avoid passing your life, thinking about other times, and not actually living the life that you were designed to live.

As you go through this book, you will be shown different ways in which you can bring mindfulness into your life. You will also be shown how to maximize the experience of being mindful. This occurs not only when you meditate but in every action that you do each day and when you learn to be mindful, you become much happier because your mind is no longer filled with all the baggage from the past or the worries from the future. It is too busy enjoying this moment in time.

The idea of Buddhist philosophy is that if you follow what is called the Eight Fold Path, you become more contented in your life. Although this book does not go into depth on the subject of Buddhist philosophy, it is necessary that you know why it came into existence. Many years before the birth of Christ, a young prince decided to venture out into the world and had been protected for so many years within the walls of his father's palace. When he noticed how much mankind suffered, he pondered on how this could be improved and why human beings suffer and the Noble Eight Fold path was the result of his enlightenment or the ideas that he came up with to try and make people suffer less. Mindfulness is just one of the paths that make up the Noble Eightfold path and it is still helping people today as much as it did back in the days when the philosophy was founded.

Chapter 4: What Is Meditation?

Our modern world is so overwhelming from economic pressure and family and work demands to technological challenges that upset our natural balance. The overload in no time overwhelms and overloads your mind leading to stress, fear, depression, and anxiety. People often spend almost 50 percent of their working hours thinking about issues that aren't what they're doing, a mind-wandering experience that make them unhappy. And though such behavior comes at an emotional cost; such mind-wandering is, unfortunately, the brain's mode of operation!

So what happens next? The negative information fed to the brain with time results into negative thoughts, which explains why we most often focus on negative incidents. Research has shown that around 95 percent of our thoughts are repetitive, with 80 percent being negative. The good news is that practicing meditation has helped many people to calm their minds and obtain inner peace. That said; being mindful doesn't necessarily mean that you stop thinking, but it helps surpass thinking as opposed to suppressing it. When you concentrate on your body, a mantra or just your breathing, negative thoughts come and go just like the clouds across the sky. So what exactly is meditation?

Simply put, meditation is a broad variety of practices aimed at helping you get more relaxed, promote self-awareness, and build inner strength, compassion, or love. When you meditate and are mindful, it's easier to realize how your thinking affects your emotions, and this can eventually help you fight negative emotions. The practice also helps improve focus and makes you aware when your attention drifts away, and can boost your focus even when not meditating. Without relaxation techniques like meditation, stress and anxiety can trigger a strong reaction in the medial prefrontal cortex of your brain and make you feel under attack.

In order to give you the motivation to start practicing meditation, it is important to understand how you stand to benefit by meditating. Let us look at some benefits of meditation in the following chapter.

Why Practice Meditation

Research has shown that meditation has very many health benefits such as deep relaxation achieved in meditation helps lower blood sugar as well as blood pressure. The biggest achievement of meditation is that you become happier! Practicing meditation places you on the fast track to happiness as it triggers brain signaling in the left side of your prefrontal cortex. The effect is linked to positive emotions, as opposed to decreasing in activity on the right side, which causes negative emotions. For people who suffer disease which brings you back to yourself, meditation can help you accept the condition. Mindfulness helps you explore your inner self and thus realize that health conditions can be overcome.

That said; let's see 5 ways in which you can actually benefit from a few minutes of a meditation session:

1. Better or improved memory

Meditation is linked to boosting memory recall. Based on a research study, people who practiced mindfulness meditation were able to control the brain wave that is involved in screening out distractions. They also increased their productivity faster compared to those who didn't meditate. The ability to ignore or surpass distractions can explain a person's superior ability to remember and incorporate new facts quickly. The exposure is similar to facing a new situation and can dramatically boost your memory on things or events.

2. Slows down the aging process

Meditating regularly has shown to boost the gray matter in the frontal cortex and hippocampus areas of the brain. The more the gray matter you have, the more you react positively to emotions, show longer-lasting emotional stability and even boost focus. Meditation also helps reduce the age-related effects on gray matter and thus hinder the decrease of your cognitive functioning.

Research findings suggest that meditation can modify your brain's physiology to slow down the aging process. People who meditate tend to have more brain cells due to higher levels of gray matter. Another research found out that meditating creates longer telomeres, the caps on chromosomes that indicate biological age (not the chronological age). Longer telomeres are linked to slow aging process or a longer life.

3. Increased immunity and fertility

Progressive muscular relaxation involved with meditation has shown to increase immunity especially in recovering cancer patients. Patients who practice mindfulness and relaxation exercises daily, reduce the risk of breast cancer reoccurring. The relaxation achieved in meditation also helps boost the natural killer cells in the elderly and thus give them a greater resistance to viruses and tumor. In addition, meditation decreases levels of stress, which in turn boosts sperm count in males, which translates to increased fertility. According to studies, women are more likely to conceive when they are relaxed as opposed to when stressed.

4. Reduces blood pressure

Meditation triggers relaxation, a process that boosts a compound known as nitric oxide that opens up blood vessels to slow down blood pressure. People who practice meditation have managed to control their blood pressure without taking medication. When you meditate, your body also becomes lesser responsive to stress hormones, in a similar manner as the medication works.

5. Helps Reduce Stress and Anxiety

Research has shown that regular meditation can help relieve stress and anxiety and restore calmness and inner peace. When you meditate, you focus your mind on things like love; and you become more aware of which things in life cause you emotional strain, stress, and anxiety. Mindful meditation has been proven to help people work under pressure but feel less stressed. Based on a study, participants who practiced meditation were more comfortable to handle a stressful multitasking task compared to those who never undertook mindfulness training.

Various changes in the brain take place when you meditate, such as the frontal lobe appearing to go offline. This part of the brain is involved with emotions, planning, reasoning and self-conscious awareness. Meditation also lowers the flow of data into the thalamus and can help you feel less alert or aroused from external stimuli.

Now that you know how you stand to benefit by meditating let us now look at some meditation techniques that you can use.

Chapter 5: The Power Of Looking Inward

A person's experience of life is mostly anchored on events and actions external to them. For example, there are plenty of people who judge their happiness according to how other people see them. Somehow, in their minds, how they feel and who they are is affected by other people's perceptions.

Everyone tends to live life according to things that are outside of themselves. They continuously analyze what other people think or are too busy trying to find external events that distract them from their own thoughts. It can be easy to become pre-occupied with everything happening around you. Meditation, however, aims to allow the individual to get back in touch with his or her own mind. This is the key to true peace.

The Essence of Meditation

You might not realize it, but your mind tends to be a restless and often times chaotic place. Traditional Buddhists used to liken the mind with a monkey that never stayed still, always hopping from one thought to another every other moment.

Being Aware of Awareness

You've probably never really paid attention to your own awareness. Your train of thought can often seem as if it's independent of you. For example, have you ever found yourself being surprised by a seemingly sudden thought that just came out of nowhere? Although it may seem like it just popped into your head, there was probably a pattern behind it, you were just too distracted to realize it.

Awareness is so significant and yet often neglected. Your awareness is part and parcel of who you are, a constant aspect of your psyche, and yet you hardly ever pay attention to it. Through meditation, you can finally get to know your own mind and trace the patterns of your thought. Only by getting to know the maps of your mind can you finally keep it still and find peace.

Paying Attention to Yourself

Since distraction and escaping reality is the most common way to deal with any negative emotions or life experiences, people don't really pay attention to their own mind. Many people who fall into a spiral of depressive thoughts find themselves unable to control it.

But before you can hope to control, you must first learn to understand. Negative emotions are never any fun, after all, who wants to feel bad? Remembering painful or humiliating events often causes a kind of reflex that suppresses these emotions and memories. Because of this, your own emotions can be a mystery to you. Meditation, however, allows you to get to know your own mind through stillness and attention.

Building Confidence and Learning Self-Love

Society, as a whole, seems to have a problem with self-acceptance. Whole industries are based on people not being contented with what they have. Being accepting and loving of yourself can be very difficult especially when you're always faced with suggestive ads showcasing perfection and societal pressures that demand submission to the norm.

Acceptance through Openness

Meditation and mindfulness require stillness of the mind through openness, not through suppression. The only way you can still your mind is by being open and accepting of your own thoughts. This acceptance is very important in developing confidence and self-love. Before you can want to be a better person or reach higher goals, you first have to be able to accept and truly love who you are at the present.

You have to see all the aspects of your being without any judgment. You must simply acknowledge your strengths and weaknesses and even appreciate them.

You have to let go of all the standards you have and just pay attention to yourself. Allow every thought to arrive and accept it without being critical of yourself. This openness to your own thoughts paves the way to acceptance and, eventually, to confidence and love.

Loving Acknowledgement

One of the main reasons you can feel neglected is because you do not acknowledge your own emotions and thoughts. This can be because you have been made to believe that thinking or being a certain way is wrong or a sign of weakness. Whatever the reason may be, not being able to acknowledge your own feelings can send a hidden message to your own psyche: your thoughts and emotions don't matter.

When you ignore, suppress, or hide your emotions, it's as if you are saying that you're not worth understanding or that you're not worth standing up for. You have to be able to acknowledge all your emotions and thoughts. For example, when a certain painful emotion arises, don't shy away from it or try to suppress it. Instead, allow the pain to flow through you and acknowledge it. Embrace the emotions and the thoughts behind them, only then can you let them go.

Marvel at Yourself

Before anything else, you have to be able to establish something: your body and mind are the miracles of life. There is so much you can do, so much potential that only needs to be tapped. In fact, everyone has the potential to do something special, be a hero, and save the day. The only reason that people feel inadequate is that they pay more attention to what others have than on themselves. People who choose to compare themselves with others will always find a reason to be disappointed.

No matter how good you are, someone else will always come along who's better than you. There will always be someone better or worse than you and comparing yourself to others will never bring you any lasting happiness. You have to learn to appreciate who you are, as you are. There is no other way. And although you may be unaware of this, there is so much about yourself that you can marvel at. For example, the simple beauty of life is already a marvel. The fact that you are the product of millions of years of evolution is already amazing.

If you simply choose to take the time, it won't take long for you to realize how truly amazing and beautiful you are.

A Change in Perspective: Focus and Mental Power

Focused awareness is of utmost importance when it comes to meditation. You can't simply be aware. You also have to be able to focus your attention on your awareness rather than letting you attention wander towards random thoughts.

Unlocking Concentration

This age of distractions can make concentration very difficult. There is just too much stimulation in the world so that the little monkey that is your mind doesn't really know where to look. However, in order to do anything well, you must learn how to concentrate and focus on a certain activity.

Learning to develop strong concentration demands mental training that can be achieved through meditation. Sitting quietly isn't just about stillness, but also about focus and attention. When you meditate, you are training your mind to stay focused on your awareness and develop stronger powers of concentration.

Getting into the Flow through Focused Awareness

The flow is a state of extreme concentration where people often lose track of time as they engage in a certain activity. This means that all your attention was focused on one thing and many people often surprise themselves with what they are able to do.

In order to get into the flow, you have to be able cultivate unswerving concentration and focused awareness, a basic concept in meditation. Meditation and mindfulness allow you to diminish any distractions and direct your awareness to a certain activity.

The Joy in Mindfulness

Mindfulness is a special meditation technique that focuses on awareness of the present. It is all about learning to live from moment to moment and becoming totally engaged in things as they happen rather than by being distracted by the past, the present or made-up fantasies.

The Gift of the Present

What else do we have if not the present? Since there's nothing to be done about the past and there's no concrete way to predict the future, all we really have is the present. After all, isn't life just a series of present moments coming one after the other?

Then why is it often so hard to pay attention to it? Why are so many people living life so distractedly? There are so many people who take the present for granted, thinking that they will always have more time. The truth, however, is that the only thing you can lose that can never be earned back is the time that is wasted.

How many people have dinner with their families and are just zoned out the entire time, or go on vacation and still constantly worry about work or home? All these "mentally absent" moments are wasted because they just went by unnoticed. Mindfulness reminds you to take each moment and savor its essence, to find joy and wholesome pleasure from simple, everyday things.

Simply by taking a little time every day for a meditation practice, you are effectively developing your awareness. Through meditation, you are getting to know yourself and unlocking your own happiness.

Chapter 6: The 'Why' Of Mindfulness

You might have asked yourself this question already: why is it all that important to be mindful? Well, let's take a look at all the most wonderful benefits that mindfulness can afford us, before we delve deeper into understanding exactly how we can employ mindfulness techniques to our best possible advantage.

The top 10 benefits of mindfulness

1 Mindfulness meditation helps to alleviate anxiety and depression

Of course one would expect their stress levels to be reduced through the process of meditation, but mindfulness meditation takes things a few notches higher by helping people who are undergoing anxiety and depression, to alleviate their symptoms by a great extent. All the more reason, then, to employ the art of mindfulness meditation if you are suffering from anxiety or depression.

2 It helps in an objective analysis of oneself.

You will find that a lot of times we view ourselves as being perfect, but that view of ourselves is far removed from reality and once we can look at ourselves through the glasses of mindfulness we will find that we gain a far clearer and true perspective of ourselves. This can help us deal with several issues that we might be grappling with, through the process of understanding our flaws and allowing us to see the necessity to change. At the very same time, being mindful will help ensure that we don't fall into the trap of exemplifying our flaws and causing us a whole lot of undue grief in the process.

#3 It helps to achieve a greater degree of focus.

When you start being mindful, you will find that you are able to achieve a far greater degree of focus in your everyday life than you otherwise would have. You will be able to concentrate on important tasks without petty distractions coming in your way, and thus emerge as a far more efficient person in the process.

#4 It helps you be more creative.

Creativity is the one thing that can take us places. You will find that as you get more and more mindful, your creativity levels get bolstered by a good deal. This is because your mind is completely de cluttered in the process of striving to be mindful, and an uncluttered mind is of paramount importance where it comes to being creative!

#5 It helps us enjoy music better.

According to a study done in the journal Psychology of Music, mindfulness can help enrich our experience of music. If we love listening to music, we will find ourselves enjoying it a lot more when we become more and more mindful over time. This is achieved because we get to be far more engaged in the process of listening to music, when we are mindful.

#6 It helps with your relationship.

If you are in a relationship with someone, you are of course privy to stressful situations that emerge every now and then where it comes to your partner,

and the good thing about mindfulness is that it helps you deal and cope with these emotionally draining times in a much better manner, by helping you to react better to that relationship stress as well as communicate your emotions better to your partner.

#7 Mindfulness is great for reducing addictive, self-destructive behavior.

In the case of people abusing illegal or prescription drugs and/or alcohol, mindfulness plays a pivotal role in reducing such self-destructive behavior to a great extent.

#8 It actually makes you a better person.

According to a study in the journal Psychological Science, mindfulness meditation can actually help make you a better person, by making us a lot more compassionate than we already are.

Therefore, we will find that if we are mindful we will certainly exhibit a better behavior than we already do, and even go out of our way to help those in need.

#9 It helps you get that beauty sleep at night.

A lot of our problems can be solved if we simply get enough sleep at night, and by incorporating mindfulness into your life you will be able to do just that. This in turn keeps you all the more primed to mange any future stress that might be coming your way, in the best possible manner. All the more reason, then, to make mindfulness a part of your lifestyle!

#10 It helps you become less emotionally reactive.

There are things that happen in life that one is completely unprepared for – like the attack on the Twin Towers so many years ago. Being mindful helps you cope better with sudden stressful events that might actually cause a good deal of grief in people not emotionally strong enough to deal with such stressors that might emerge out of the blue.

Chapter 7: Origin Of Mindfulness

The practice of what we today know as mindfulness began about 2500 years ago amongst the Buddhists. The root word for Mindfulness is "sati" which roughly translates to memory in the Brahman language. It refers to the early practice adopted by the Brahmans where they cleared their mind of all distractions and side thoughts before beginning to memorize a scripture.

This practice was adopted by Buddha in his quest for inner peace. Instead of memorizing texts, he used it to achieve connectivity with the soul of the world during meditation.

Most of the modern notions about Mindfulness are derived from the vipassanāvāda which talks of mindfulness (or satipatthana as it is referred in the texts) as a form of meditation where the person achieves a sense of clarity by simply being mindful of the activities and changes around him.

However this is just one most common interpretation of the vipassanāvāda. Different schools of thought differ on what exactly constitutes the practice of satipatthana. There are about seven different adaptations of the same text.

Sati and upatthana are the root words for satipatthana. These translate to 'setting up' or 'establishing'. Which means that the person practicing the technique becomes more aware of the presence of himself and other objects in the realm of the universe

Satipatthana's school of thought links back to a shared ancestor. The ancient root text has been derived in various ways by different students, scholars and practitioners. Schools of thought began to form and differ from each other right after Buddha's death. Pali Abhidhamma Vibhanga is perhaps the most unaltered version of all the texts available today.

However it is also much more difficult to understand and implement. Hence most practitioners bend towards other simpler texts for guidance.

This simplicity arises from the gradual change that occurred over the ages. The samatha aspect of the satiphatthana was given priority while the vipassana aspect was gradually reduced. This major change is common amongst all schools of thought that evolved the text with time. Resultantly this caused various disagreements in the process of interpretation.

However despite the differences, the basic soul and aim of the satiphatthana remains uniform across all schools of thought.

The practice of satiphatthana made its way to the West first via Vivekananda whose distinctive and personalized interpretations of the text were very well received by the Western audience. The guidelines of the practice also became widely accessible after the Pali Text Society translated the Buddhist Sutras to

English. However it was during the 19th century that the Eastern concept of meditation first grasped its roots in the Western world. This was through the works of D. T. Suzuki who presented a practical interpretation that was more suited to the Western lifestyle.

Mindfulness-Based Stress Reduction (MBSR) Program was formed at the University of Massachusetts in 1979 by Jon Zin. The program was aimed at giving a relief to those who were fatally sick. Owing to the great response to Mindfulness-Based Stress Reduction Program, similar concepts to MBSR are now in function at various community centres such as prisons, schools and hospitals.

Studying the historical approach of mindfulness and tracing its evolution through various schools of thought, help us get a more pronounced and clear understanding of the practice. By referring to the authentic text we can gain a more productive, practical and soulful idea of the tradition of satiphatthana.

Chapter 8: What Is Meditation?

What is meditation? Meditation has been used in a variety of religions since man first started asking the "big questions." Whether it was Buddhism, Christianity, Daoism, Hinduism, Islam, Judaism, New age or even the Occult, mankind has practiced religion and has also practiced meditation. My intention when beginning The Mastery of Meditation is to bring the joys of meditation to as many people as possible. I want to help people. While meditation is generally taken to be a deeply religious practice (and the techniques in this book can certainly add to the quality of your worship) I would like it to be known that almost every major religion either currently practices, or has practiced, some form of meditation and that the practices within are good for everyone, regardless of religious affiliation or belief system. It is just as good for a Jew as it is for an atheist or a polytheist. No matter who you are, or what you believe, or what you have done in the past, opening this book is beginning a path in your life that can lead to something beautiful. Stick with meditation, and it will reward you in amazing ways.

What Meditation is, as simply put as possible, is the focused training of the mind to produce a beneficial result. People who meditate find themselves with lower stress, better focus, and higher mental stamina. Lesser known effects of daily meditation include a more full and deep insight into who you are, what your experiences mean and how you react to your senses as well as more full understanding of your emotions and the relationship between your consciousness and those emotions.

The long answer is that meditation (over a period of time) is the ability to exist within reality, the way that it stands, outside of our own constant inner monologue. A good practice can help you to focus intensely and to see things for how they truly are, as opposed to viewing them through the skewed lenses of our own inner judgment. We all have preconceived notions about life that evolved within us after a lifetime of experiences have pressed on us. Our experiences force us to view the world in a different way, and to approach life from a different point of view. This isn't always a bad thing, but the lessons that we learn tend to bleed over to other aspects of life. If a parent betrayed us early on, then we might learn to distrust all authority. If a loved one breaks our heart, then we might hesitate to love again or even search endlessly for someone to fill the gap left behind. When things happen to us, good or bad, we get lost in the ensuing emotions. This is human nature, to constantly take in stimuli and turn it into something meaningful. Our brains are amazing in that ability to get lost in something which exists only within the mind, whether that is an emotion, or a memory, or a future event. This isn't something arguable, it happens to all of us every single day. Take yourself, for example; have you ever found yourself, when you are at home alone, arguing with someone who isn't there? Pacing back and forth working yourself up because you "just know" what they are going to say? Have you ever pulled into a parking spot at work, having driven 20 or more minutes, to find yourself wondering what you were just thinking about, or not able to remember the drive at all? Meditation can be our navigator through this sea of distractibility. It can help us to hone our minds into focused machines capable of sidestepping unnecessary pre-judgments and stresses so that we can face the reality of our current situations with a full and honest view of how things really are, right now. Meditation creates the ability to suspend your inner dialogue and focus not on your emotional baggage, or your interpretation of the moment, but to exist in the present and see it unfolding in front of you without judgment. This ability is life changing in so many positive ways. I can't wait for you to find out how!

Chapter 9: Why Meditation Is Good For You?

You frequently hear that reflection is the way to achievement. You regularly get notification from individuals, particularly the top competitors or the top experts in their own particular industry, say that without a type of reflection, they would not be the place they are presently. Its is by all accounts that history has recorded that the best people have had some type of reflection or perception on their side, or some type of contemplation activity, to help them accomplish their objectives.

In any case, why would that be? Why do we have to find this lost craftsmanship, which the self improvement group is so widespread about, to accomplish our objectives? Also, do we have enough time?

You see, melancholy and emotional instability has expanded throughout the most recent couple of decades. Indeed, the most concerning thing is that we live in an exceptionally discouraged and worried world. Also, accordingly, more individuals are going to see a councilor or an advisor to have help with respect to their mental uneasiness or condition, in spite of being on a planet which should be innovatively and socially progressed.

Would it be able to be, that we are working too hard as an animal types? Would it be able to be that we are over depleting ourselves, that we are making decidedly a lot of move at work, that we are getting far excessively worried effectively. Is this what is bringing on the psychological well-being issues?

All things considered, we will never know without a doubt, however what we do know is that a decent approach to help yourself is through the craft of contemplation. Only 5 minutes previously, then after the fact going to bed is everything you need, that is all it takes. Be that as it may, why is contemplation so essential?

There are numerous reasons why thinking is beneficial for you. One of the principle reasons is that its really an extremely self-recuperating activity. Also, this is the reason individuals who do ruminate over a consistent premise, wind up feeling all the more better with the world. It really helps resolve, or if nothing else recuperate old, passionate issues or issues. This is on the grounds that it helps candidly disengage, to a degree, old recollections so you feel all the more better about what the past injury was.

Also, you don't get excessively affected by the past. You have the capacity to have a clearer head and think all the more suitably. You get the opportunity to improve more, educated choices identifying with your issue nearby. You have the capacity to think all the more obviously and feel all the more candidly adjusted.

Thirdly, you get the chance to collaborate all the more gently and congruously towards other individuals. So you are not fast to get furious or upset, you are all the more sincerely smooth, and you get the opportunity to mingle all the more viably, so its better all round.

Yet, one of the best preferences, is that it assists with the law of fascination. Furthermore, you've frequently heard by the self improvement group that reflection assists with the law of fascination, on the grounds that it helps you be in a state which permits you to get more plenitude, and more bliss, without needing to make a considerable measure of move. So it helps in such a variety of diverse ways.

Chapter 10: 12 Indispensable Mindful Living Tools

The focus of my life in recent months has been living mindfully, and while I don't always remember to do that, I have learned a few things worth sharing.

The first is a mindful life is worth the effort. It's a life where we awaken from the dream state we're most often submerged in — the state of having your mind anywhere but the present moment, locked in thoughts about what you're going to do later, about something someone else said, about something you're stressing about or angry about. The state of mind where we're lost in our smartphones and social media.

It's worth the effort, because being awake means we're not missing life as we walk through it. Being awake means we're conscious of what's going on inside us, as it happens, and so can make more conscious choices rather than acting on our impulses all the time.

The second thing I've learned is that we forget. We forget, over and over, to be awake. And that's OK. Being mindful is a process of forgetting, and then remembering. Repeatedly. Just as breathing is a process of exhaling, and then inhaling, repeatedly.

The third is that mindful living isn't just one thing. It's not just meditation. Nor is it just focusing on the sensations around you, right now in this moment. I've found mindful living to be a set of very related tools, perhaps all different ways of getting at the same thing, but each useful in its own regard.

I'll share them in this post, and hope that you'll consider each in turn.

Why You Should Care

Why bother to spend the time learning these tools? Is it just for some ideal of living a peaceful, stress-free life?

No. A stress-free life doesn't exist, but these tools will definitely make you more prepared to deal with the stresses that will inevitably come your way.

But just as importantly, they'll help you overcome the fear of failure and fear of discomfort that's holding you back, that's keeping you from making positive changes in your life.

These tools will help you launch your new blog, start a business, write a book, put out your first music album online, find your purpose in life, become the person you've always wanted to be.

This is what I've found. I'm certain you'll find these tools just as useful.

The Toolset

This list, of course, is not complete. It's a collection of things I've been learning about, and am still practicing, things I've found useful enough to share.

Meditation. Meditation is where mindful living starts. And it's not complicated: you can sit still for even just 1 minute a day to start with (work up to 3-5 minutes after a week), and turn your attention to your body and then your breath. Notice when your thoughts wander from your breath, and gently return to the breath. Repeat until the minute is up. Let accept "Do Nothing 'Can You Do That'" chalenge at your Peace Starter Meditation app, You can just focus on meditation without thinking about keeping track of time.

Be Awake. Meditation is practice for being awake, which is not being in the dream state (mind wandering into a train of thought, getting lost in the online world, thinking about past offenses, stressing about the future, etc.) but being awake to the present, to what is. Being awake is something you can do throughout the day, all the time, if you remember. Remembering is the trick.

Watch Urges. When I quit smoking in 2014, the most useful tool I learned was watching my urges to smoke. I would sit there and watch the urge rise and fall, until it was gone, without acting on it. It taught me that I am not my urges, that I don't have to act on my urges, and this helped me change all my other habits. Watch your urge to check email or social media, to eat something sweet or fried, to drink alcohol, to watch TV, to be distracted, to procrastinate. These urges will come and go, and you don't have to act on them.

Watch Ideals. We all have ideals, all the time. We have an ideal that our day will go perfectly, that people will be kind and respectful to us, that we will be perfect, that we'll ace an exam or important meeting, that we'll never fail. Of course, we know from experience that those ideals are not real, that they don't come true, that they aren't realistic. But we still have them, and they cause our stress and fears and grief over something/someone we've lost. By letting go of ideals, we can let go of our suffering.

Accept People & Life As They Are. When I stopped trying to change a loved one, and accepted him for who he was, I was able to just be with him and enjoy my time with him. This acceptance has the same effect for anything you do — accept a co-worker, a child, a spouse, but also accept a "bad" situation, an unpleasant feeling, an annoying sound. When we stop trying to fight the way things are, when we accept what is, we are much more at peace.

Let Go of Expectations. This is really the same thing as the previous two items, but I've found it useful nonetheless. It's useful to watch your expectations with an upcoming situation, with a new project or business, and see that it's not real and that it's causing you stress and disappointment. We cause our own pain, and we can relieve it by letting go of the expectations that are causing it. Toss your expectations into the ocean.

Become OK with Discomfort. The fear of discomfort is huge — it causes people to be stuck in their old bad habits, to not start the business they want to start, to be stuck in a job they don't really like, because we tend to stick to the known and comfortable rather than try something unknown and uncomfortable. It's why many people don't eat vegetables or exercise, why they eat junk, why they don't start something new. But we can be OK with discomfort, with practice. Start with things that are a little uncomfortable, and keep expanding your comfort zone.

Watch Your Resistance. When you try to do something uncomfortable, or try to give up something you like or are used to, you'll find resistance. But you can just watch the resistance, and be curious about it. Watch your resistance to things that annoy you — a loud sound that interrupts your concentration, for example. It's not the sound that's the problem, it's your resistance to the sound. The same is true of resistance to food we don't like, to being too cold or hot, to being hungry. The problem isn't the sensation of the food, cold, heat or hunger — it's our resistance to them. Watch the resistance, and feel it melt. This resistance, by the way, is why I'm doing my Year of Living Without.

Be Curious. Too often we are stuck in our ways, and think we know how things should be, how people are. Instead, be curious. Find out. Experiment. Let go of what you think you know. When you start a new project or venture, if you feel the fear of failure, instead of thinking, "Oh no, I'm going to fail" or "Oh no, I don't know how this will turn out", try thinking, "Let's see. Let's find out." And then there isn't the fear of failure, but the joy of being curious and finding out. Learn to be OK with not knowing.

Be Grateful. We complain about everything. But life is a miracle. Find something to be grateful about in everything you do. Be grateful when you're doing a new habit, and you'll stick to it longer. Be grateful when you're with someone, and you'll be happier with them. Life is amazing, if you learn to appreciate it.

Let Go of Control. We often think we control things, but that's only an illusion. Our obsession with organization and goals and productivity, for example, are rooted in the illusion that we can control life. But life is uncontrollable, and just when we think we have things under control, something unexpected comes up to disrupt everything. And then we're frustrated because things didn't go the way we wanted. Instead, practice letting go of control, and learn to flow.

Be Compassionate. This sounds trite, but compassion for others can change the way you feel about the world, on a day-to-day basis. And compassion for yourself is life-changing. These two things need remembering, though, so mindful living is about remembering to be compassionate after you forget.

Open your Peace Starter Meditation app and go Universe Meditation section wheever you want to "Accept People & Life As They Are", "Let Go of Expectations"," Become OK with Discomfort"," Watch Your Resistance"," Be Grateful" and "Let Go of Control". Also this help clear your mind and Hope you feel a little less stressed and a little more connected

Chapter 11: Applying These Techniques To Everyday Situations

There are new students who tell me that they don't have time for relaxation or for meditation. In fact we examined the kind of things that they do in their lives and one of the greatest time consumers was driving a car. Of course, meditation and driving are not really wise combinations since you need full attention on the driving itself, but that's not to say that mindfulness cannot play a part. That's one of the wonderful things about mindfulness. It doesn't matter what you are doing. You can still do it safely and use mindfulness to make the experience even more enjoyable.

How many readers drive the car with the sound turned fully on and then have to open the window to let the sound out? The reason that you do this is because you are pushing too much sound into your mind and it becomes too busy to function correctly. Next time you are tempted to open the window to let the sound out, try this. Turn off the radio and listen to the relative silence. Instantly, this boosts the way that you feel. How can you be aware of any muscular pain or tension in your body and help to relax it if you are flooding your senses with other things?

Once the radio is turned off, tune in to your body and the parts of your body that need your attention. Do you have an aching neck? Do you have a knotted stomach? Do you have legs which hurt because of the position they are in? Once you are mindful of your body's needs, you can begin to address these, even while you are driving.

Of course you cannot do meditation in the true sense of the word because you need to be concentrating on your driving. Your life and the lives of others depend upon it. However, you can be mindful. If you leg is cramped from being in the wrong position, stretch it out and help it to become more comfortable. If you need to stop the car and adjust the seat, then find a safe spot and do this. Until you turned off the radio, you were not even aware of the pain being caused to your leg.

If you find that you do have a knot in the stomach, try breathing exercises, followed by pulling the muscles of the stomach in or "Pumping" the muscles until they feel a little more relaxed. You can effectively do that while you are driving without taking attention from the road.

Take note of how you react to driving manouvers

Do you sit behind the wheel getting frustrated because you have a commercial vehicle in front of you? Do you feel yourself getting more and more stressed because you cannot find a place to overtake? This is all adding to stress. Slow down. There is no need for driving to be so competitive. When you do slow down, you allow your heart beat to slow down as well and you allow your body to release all that negative tension.

Take pleasure from opportunities

When traffic permits, be aware of those around you. It's always great driving practice to have all round visibility but many people don't even use it. Be aware of the old lady trying to cross the road. Be polite and friendly to other drivers even if they do something that annoys you. The point is that they made the mistake and you don't have to live that mistake and make the negativity part of who you are. When you do that, you lose mindfulness and take on the stance of criticism and that's negative stuff.

The reason that driving was shown as the typical example is because most people have to do this and spend a lot of time in their cars. Once they learn that they can be mindful at the same time as doing something as complex as driving, it's easy to apply that to other areas of life.

Chapter 12: Mindfulness

To put a definition to mindfulness; I will define it as the act of paying attention to our thoughts and feelings. In other words, it is a state of consciousness that includes awareness and attention. We all have a mind, which is where all of our thoughts emanate from. However, most of us are not in control of our mind, rather our mind is in control of us. Do you know that what you think about the most can put a limitation to your potentials or can give your imaginations the wings to fly?

Mindfulness presupposes that although many thoughts scale through your mind, you are careful what thoughts to accept. The mind is like a formula one car on a track way, it is always racing and it is always racing as long as you are not asleep or dead, however, it is entirely left to you what you allow to settle in your mind. It is apt that I used the example of a formula one car earlier, just as a car needs maintenance, the mind also needs maintenance. By maintenance, I mean scrutinizing your thought process, what you think and how you think. You must fill your mind with positive thoughts and deliberately skip negative thoughts from your consciousness.

We cannot effectively discuss mindfulness without speaking on self-awareness. Self-awareness is simply paying attention to our own emotions, doing this will enable us to understand ourselves better including our habits and why we seem to enjoy indulging in them. Self-awareness is a relevant endeavor because it enables the individual to be able to monitor thoughts and emotions as they arise. The mind is primed on storing information; self-awareness brings us into the knowledge of the preconceptions of the mind. However, as important as self-awareness is, the truth is that most of us are really conscious of ourselves because most of the time, the mind operates on the unconscious.

It is a proven fact that mindfulness improves productivity, health and general well-being. Furthermore, the best way to boost mindfulness is through meditation. Here are some tips on how to improve your level of mindfulness;

Breathing and Concentration: Breathing is connected to meditation and mindfulness. When you deliberately breathe in and out there is an interruption in your mind concerning whatever you are doing and the mind pays attention to your breathing. Breathing exercises bring about an interaction in the mental discourse going on in the mind and the limelight is now beamed on the breath. For effectiveness, you may associate the in-breath and the out-breath, this will all the more improved. The length of your in-breath is the length of your mindfulness.

Body awareness: It is possible that a student went to school to attend a lecture and then after the lecture, you ask the same student, what the lecture of that day was all about, it is possible that the student may not be able to say anything meaningful or logical because he or she was just physically present in class but their mind was miles away from the classroom. As you breathe in and out solemnly, picture yourself in a cool, relaxed atmosphere and your body is relaxed.

Releasing tension: When you truly reach the state of body awareness, you will realize there are some pains occasioned by stress in the body. To release the pent up tension in your body, breathe in my mindfully saying these words as you breathe in "am aware of my body" and mindfully utter this words "I release the tension in my body" as you breathe out. Please note that by mindfully utter, I imply that you don't speak the words with a mouth but just imagine saying the words as you breathe in and out.

Chapter 13: So What Is This Mindfulness All About?

Mindfulness is the deliberate, accepting and unprejudiced focus of the attention of an individual on his emotions, opinions and sensations happening in the present time. It can be taught by meditational exercises derived from Buddhist anapanasati.

Technically, mindfulness is a derivative of an essential component of Buddhist training. It is a practice employed to alleviate a wide array of mental and bodily conditions in the field of psychology. It had been found effective for treating obsessive-compulsive disorder, stress and anxiety; in the deterrence of relapse in depression and addiction; and in handling emotions in general.

Mindfulness is currently achieving a growing acceptance as a practice in everyday life, separate from the Buddhist insight thought and its application in the practice of psychology. It is now seen as a way of being, and can be experienced outside a ceremonial setting.

It is described as a moment-by-moment consciousness of the environment, thoughts, physical sensations and feelings, distinguished mainly by a person's acceptance or attentiveness to feelings and thoughts without considering whether they are wrong or right.

Mindfulness converges the brain on what is being picked up at every moment, instead of on its usual rumination on yesterday or on tomorrow. The "Mindfulness Movement" has come into the mainstream, essentially through the effort of Jon Kabat-Zinn and his

Mindfulness-Based Stress Reduction (MBSR) program, launched at the University of Massachusetts Medical School in 1979.[1]

For almost 35 years, scientific studies have authenticated the mental and physical health assistance of MBSR and mindfulness. Programs founded on MBSR and parallel models have been extensively adapted in learning institutions, prisons, hospices, veteran centers and other settings.

Jon Kabat-Zinn claims that the exercise of mindfulness may be beneficial to a variety of people in Western society who might be reluctant to adopt Buddhist practices. Western scholars and clinicians who have presented the exercise of mindfulness into mental wellness treatment instructions usually instill these skills separately of its cultural and religious background. But is being attentive to the present moment really difficult? Sadly, yes. Let us be honest to ourselves. Is it not true that, in many instances, we go through what we do in a routine manner while our thoughts wander to past or future events?

How about those moments when we just allow our mind to wander? These drifting thoughts generally involve anger, self-pity, cravings, revenge, sadness, worries and fears. And in so doing, we really are not into the present. What makes it worse though is the power of these thoughts to reinforce reactions and sentiments which all boil down to unhappiness.

Why then can we not pay attention to the present moment? We can come up with a thousand and one reasons but no reason can defend the importance of "now" – the "now" which will be tomorrows thoughts being past, the "now" with all its potential for a better tomorrow.

Thus, in mindfulness, we are involved with noticing what is going on "now." But then again, it does not mean we should not reflect on yesterday and tomorrow. It only means that, when we do so, we should be mindful or completely aware of our thoughts.

In reality, mindfulness is a technique of meditation. The difference though is that, in meditation, the concern is with what is arising in the "now" moment. In mindfulness, awareness of drifting thoughts are controlled by bringing them back to the "now" moment.

By deliberately directing our attentiveness away from drifting thoughts and bringing them back to the present time, we decrease their influence on our lives and we make, instead, a breathing space where tranquility and contentment can grow.

Mindfulness is an expressively non-reactive instance. We do not give a verdict if the moment is positive or negative for us. And should we have a verdict, we simply acknowledge and release it with no reaction at all. We merely accept anything that comes our way observing it mindfully and without judgment.

We see it coming, happening and fading away like a passive observer. Whether it is an enjoyable or a pain-filled experience, we treat it in a similar way. This process involves the brain recognizing events but not allowing emotions to get in the way.

Chapter 14: Why Mindfulness Is A Good Place To Start

What does it look like to be mindful?

The term "mindful" is perhaps a bit misleading, as the state we're talking about isn't about identifying with the **mind** at all. When you are mindful, every one of your senses is alert, awake and aware. Your consciousness is fully engaged and receptive to the present moment as it unfolds all around you. It isn't trapped in the past or ruminating over the future, it only lives in the constantly refreshing here-and-now.

When you are mindful, you are super focused, yet calm. You feel in control of your thoughts, rather than at the mercy of them. Life seems to move more slowly somehow, with more grace and fluidity, more serenity. In this state of mind, you even occasionally experience sensations of deep bliss and well-being.

Sounds great, but so what?

Let's imagine Leah again, this time 6 months later and after she's done some intensive work on becoming more mindful of her body, her emotions and her never-ending torrent of thoughts.

She wakes up, and the first thing she does is stretch to wake up her body, noticing every tiny twinge and area of tension. She faces each challenge of the day with a sense of calm and good humor. When she is overstressed at work, she notices immediately that her shoulders are tightening, that she is communicating less effectively. She deliberately chooses to step back, take a breath and become aware of what's in her heart and mind. When she steps back, she can engage fully again later. She feels satisfied with her performance.

She is more familiar now with her inner landscape, and realizes the true sources of her stress. She works more quickly now and without interruptions and distractions. She finally listens to her body and takes herself to the doctor – an ulcer!

— and she decides to consciously learn which foods aren't agreeing with her. When she arrives at home in the evening, she immediately connects with her family. She is aware of a growing sense of dissatisfaction around mindlessly watching TV. By being mindful, she discovers that a family walk after dinner makes her feel infinitely more relaxed and fulfilled.

She journals at the end of each day, tapping into her emotions, her goals and the areas she still needs to improve. Because she's gained this deeper insight, she's able to share it with those around her, who respond positively. As she falls asleep that night, she is filled with a deep sense of calm and peace. Her life isn't really much different, honestly, but **she's** different.

She's there, alive, breathing and experiencing it all. She is "tuned in." Instead of feeling like life is rushing her by, she gets lost in a simple moment while washing dishes — as she immerses in the fullness of the moment around her, enjoys the silky feeling of the soap bubbles on her skin and the silvery glint of the water, it feels like eternity to her. And it is.

The journey to the present moment

Mindfulness is something that is deceptively simple on its face. What could be more obvious and natural than being in the moment, experiencing the world with your full consciousness? Well, it turns out that human beings are really good at **not** doing that.

Many of us are trapped in little bubbles of our own creation. We talk endlessly to ourselves through our thoughts, eventually becoming convinced that these stories are the same as reality. We are reactionary and fickle, swayed in all directions by fleeting emotions, always moving from one distraction to the other.

Mindlessness is a little like your soul having ADHD. It's all the mental gymnastics your mind goes through to avoid sitting with the present moment, as it is. The problem: there is nothing else beside the present moment! Think about it. Dwelling on the past or the future, endlessly chattering to yourself mentally, this takes you out of the moment and **out of reality**.

You feel ungrounded, inconsequential. Time evaporates somehow - you weren't there when it happened, remember? Your emotions and your body move seemingly of their own accord, with no say from you.

To get back to the present moment, to ask your mind to forget about its mental gymnastics for a while – well, this is hard work. It takes time to become acquainted with reality again – actual reality, not reality as it is through your inner stories and mental chatter. It takes bravery to face what **is**. Paradoxically, it can take a lot of effort to stop putting in so much effort!

In this next section, we'll look at some proven techniques to start your own journey back to the present moment. In a way, these exercises are about UNlearning things you've spent a life time learning.

Before we begin, keep the following in mind:

·It isn't a competition. There is no race, and there really is no way to fail. As long as you keep going, you're doing it "right."

·It's important to be consistent. Try to practice some of these exercises **every day**, rather than just here and there.

·Don't take these exercises, or yourself, too seriously. If something works, great. If it doesn't, that's also great. Stay open and curious.

·Don't worry if you encounter difficulties. You may feel bored, agitated or even sad doing some of these. This isn't a sign you've failed. It's all grist for the mill. Keep going.

Chapter 15: What Is Meditation?

Meditation is an approach used to train the mind much like the way that we use fitness to train our bodies. Through the use of meditation you can learn how to give your brain a workout helping to keep it healthy and performing at its best.

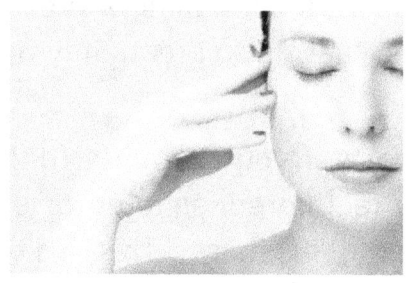

There are so many things in life that are beyond our control but we can take responsibility for our minds and learn to change them for the better through the practice of meditation. Buddhism believes this is the most important thing that we can do and is the real antidote for our own personal fears, sorrows, anxieties as well as other general confusions that affect the human condition.

Transforming the mind. Meditation is a way for us to transform our minds. The practices and techniques of Buddhist meditation help to encourage and develop emotional positivity, clarity, concentration, and a calm view of the true nature of things in the world.

You will learn the patterns and habits of your mind by engaging in particular meditation practices. Meditation will offer you new ways to cultivate more positive ways of living and being. By regularly using meditation you can become deeply focused into profoundly peaceful and energized states of mind and soul. You can go through a major transformation, which can lead to a whole new understanding and outlook on life.

Finding Inner Peace & Contentment. We all want nothing more in life than to find happiness and avoid suffering. We spend most of our time and energy in life seeking happiness, satisfaction and peace.

In the rush to seeking out these wants do we ever stop to really understand where the real source of happiness and well-being lies? Is it somewhere out in the ever-changing world we live or is it within our own minds?

We are constantly surrounded with alluring and seductive messages in our society telling and showing us the way to happiness is in money, fame, possessions, and good looks. The trouble with these options is they never seem to lead to lasting happiness. Just by taking a look around you and see how depression, stress, anxiety and loneliness are becoming more and more common along with our constant desire and need for more things.

This greed for more things is causing us to constantly take from our world and not give anything back, which is threatening the survival of our planet.

Outer or Inner Riches? When taking a closer look you will see that there are two kinds of happiness: one that is based around physical comfort and another that comes from deep within in the form of mental contentment. Many of us in this world today spend most of our waking hours in life trying to accumulate more material or "outer wealth."

There is little to no time devoted to cultivate "inner wealth", in qualities such as patience and compassion towards others and ourselves. But if we can focus on and learn how to find inner peace and contentment even when we may find ourselves facing some hardships in life we in our minds will still be happy. This can help us to understand why there are people that seem to have everything at least in "outer wealth" but yet they still seem unhappy and discontented in life compared to others that always seem content even when faced with hardships or challenges in life.

Chapter 16: Why We Are Unhappy: We Are Unhappy Because We Are Forgetful

Depression, stress, unhappiness, aggression, dissatisfaction, disappointment, envy, anger, tension, anxiety, restlessness, and loss- all these are negative conditions, emotions, and feelings all of us go through in our lives. Some of us are strong enough to battle them and move past these issues.

However, things are not always that easy for everyone, which is why many of us unsuccessfully and continuously face these issues without making any headway and soon succumb to their intense influences on our lives.

The question that goes through your mind if you are one of the 'not-so strong people' (always show reluctance towards calling anyone weak because everyone struggles through a different set of problems. Therefore, who are you to judge who is strong or weak) is this: "Why do I continuously experience these emotions despite my best effort and desire to be happy?"

The answer to this emotionally laced question is simple: you are unhappy and stressed because you possess a negative mindset, i.e. you often gravitate towards, and favor negative thinking.

Negative Thinking Generates Negative Emotions

The negative thoughts you experience generate the negative emotions you continue to experience; it is these unhealthy thoughts that restrict poisonous emotions from vacating your mind. How is that possible? Let us use a little visual picture to understand this.

You proposed to the love of your life, but he or she rejected you. You spent a few days locked up in your room feeling disappointed with yourself and your true love. Although this painful ordeal wounded and hurt you, you should have recovered from this blow in a couple of weeks, but you did not. Instead, you continued to ruminate on all the reasons why your 'one true love' refused to be with you. One negative thought led to another, and before you knew it, you were deeply lost in depression. Weeks turned into months and month into years; eventually, you could not come out of the depression pit.

Now consider the following; you lost the love of your life (feel free to insert an adequate reason why this happened); you grieved for a couple of weeks, and realized that it was not in your power to force someone to love you or nurture the same emotions for you as you have for them. Once this realization hit, you decided to live your life and wait for someone who would appreciate and love you.

These similar examples show the power of thought and clearly show how negative thoughts can spin a hurricane of negativity if you fail to discard them.

Negativity Makes You Forgetful

Another thing you need to understand is this: when you are in a negative frame of mind, you stop recognizing the amazing blessings, big or small, that you have in the present. You gravitate towards worrying about how things should have been, or how things failed to happen how you wanted them to, that you completely forget to focus on how things are now.

Various research studies conducted on negativity and forgetfulness have shown that we stay unhappy because we remain concerned about our past or future, instead of being aware of our present. This state of not being cognizant of all that you have in the present is known as 'forgetfulness' and it is the root cause of your unhappiness, stress, depression, anxiety and all other negative feelings corrupting your mind and poisoning your body.

Forgetfulness Fosters Depression

Forgetfulness forces your mind to involve itself in incessant, negative thinking. When you are forgetful, you feel as if you are living in the present, and feel present in the now, but in reality, you are not dwelling in the present: you are trapped in the past or maybe the future, but are definitely not in the present. In this state, you ponder on the past or the future events, which weaves a web of negativity. The more you think, the stronger your thoughts become and the stronger they get, the more pain you feel.

The act of forgetfulness is responsible for upsetting our lives. Therefore, to live happier, stress free lives, we must willingly make the decision to become less forgetful. How is this possible? To eliminate forgetfulness, we need to do its opposite: we need to be mindful by practicing mindfulness.

Let us delve deeper into mindfulness and discover how it can help us live healthier, fuller lives.

Chapter 17: Early Encounter With Meditation

I don't remember exactly but I think It goes way back when I was in **6th** grade . A friend of mine explained me how he improved his concentration by just concentrating on the flame of candle light. I thought to give it a try . I use to concentrate on the flame of the candle every evening until water welled in my eyes . I tried it for two to three months but nothing happened . My focus dint improved .

I slightly changed the method by concentrating on the dot on the wall instead of flame and saved the candles . But this method proved a failure . Then I jumped on sitting meditation where you concentrate on the breath . Sitting silently doing nothing was terrible experience . I read Monks do the sitting meditation for 18 hours a day and for 12 to 40 years and yet reaches no where . I Knew my one month meditation wont bring any result so I stopped doing it .

I gave up the idea of improving my memory for time being .Its hard to get obsessed with an idea if you don't find any material related to it . I had no books or magazinefrom which I could learn meditation and memory improvement technique .At that time I dint thought there could exist any such thing as self help section books. But I wouldn't miss any TV show related to boosting the memory power. I learned martial art and exercise improves the memory .I practiced martial art and running exercise everyday and it did showed some improvement . I was alert , more conscious and much focused in whatever I was doing . Exercise refreshes the mind by circulatingmore oxygenated blood towards the brain .

I dropped the martial art and exercise as I dint had enough time to devote towards it due to my busy schedule (This was just an excuse for my laziness). I forgot all about exercise and tried to devote myself towards the study . I wantedgood score to enter engineering college so I dint gave a thought about anything else except study . But I struggled a lot . I found it hard to concentrate on the study . I dint wanted to loose those precious 1 hour of the morning to memorize all the formulas of physics. After rationalizing enough I came to the conclusion maybe an exercise that can consume less time and yet effective can be tried.

I jumped on the yoga . Out of several methods one method that attracted me most was the shirshasan (King of all asans) Shirsh means head and asan means posture in other words standing on your head . Yoga is an ancient Indian method practiced to keep the mind and body clean and healthy . It was also used as a toolto reach towards enlightenment. Shirshasan or headstand postureallows plenty of supply oxygen rich blood to reach towards head and brain. It might have benefited nervous system but no improvement in the focus was recorded.

After getting frustrated from all physical exercise I switched to IQ books . I started solving puzzles related to improve the IQ. In the beginning it was fun but soon I lost the interest and found it boring.

I completed my school and somehow managed to enter the engineering college. Being in college felt very robotic . I had no enthusiasm and interest for engineering . Everyone was just running without giving a second thought whether the race belongs to them or not. I started questioning what is the meaning of existence ?. To earn the degree , get a job , pay the bills and then die . The whole system felt neurotic. This was the beginning of my spiritual search, to make some sense of the non sense.

Chapter 18: What Is Mindfulness?

What mindfulness is can be difficult to explain, but the idea can be extremely simple. Some of the greatest mindfulness practitioners have described it simply as "awareness." Others have lengthy dialogues about the deep and profound experience that is mindfulness. For this book I would like to start simply and build in complexity using what I have learned from various therapeutic modalities as well as research on the topic. Awareness can mean several things… Awareness of self, awareness of the environment, and awareness of others, to name a few. Being mindful (and therefore mindfulness) is defined as being aware of something important, or simply being inclined to be aware. Awareness is defined as knowing something exists, feeling/experiencing/noticing something, and understanding the world around you. If we bring these two definitions together, and take the assumption that everything in the world is in some way important, we come to the idea is that mindfulness is being openly aware of all things possible at any given moment. While this may sound daunting, it can be broken down into manageable parts. Mindfulness can be further summarized as noticing (being aware of) the environment and experiences of life, in reality as much as we can know it, being careful to avoid letting bias or judgment alter our perception.

After you read the next few sentences, try this exercise. Look away from the book and look up at your ceiling or look up at sky or trees or whatever is above you. Looking up is something that humans can do naturally but many of us rarely do. We often find ourselves looking at the ground in front of us as we quickly walk along the road. But taking a moment to look up and notice those things that are grander than we are reminds us of something greater than ourselves. As you look up, take the opportunity to take a few deep breaths and simply observe things above you, looking at patterns, size, shape, and color. Go ahead...

(Assuming you did...) Excellent! (If you didn't, no excellence for you, try it.) What did you notice when you practiced this? Did you notice something you have never seen before, such as a blemish on your ceiling, a certain shape of cloud or shape of leaf? Simply being aware of something that you may have previously been unaware of, bringing your attention and awareness to things you often ignore, is an important aspect of this practice. As we go through our day we often take no notice of a vast amount of information. This is normal because our brains cannot effectively organize and interpret everything that's going on in each moment. I am reminded of the Australian Tiger Beetle. This Beetle is a contender for the fastest living creature. When this beetle "runs" it moves at a speed of about 5 miles per hour, which if it was the size of a human would be equal to nearly 500 miles per hour! What is really interesting about this beetle is that when it attacks prey by tackling it at full speed, it temporarily goes blind because its visual system is unable to process information at that speed. This can be equated to a human being asked to do several tasks at once while under stress. Imagine yourself in the situation of having to answer phones, respond to emails, send a fax, make a copy, and talk to your boss simultaneously. If this was the case, you probably wouldn't notice even if something drastic occurred. Research studies in the past have tested this and suggested that someone under extreme duress won't even notice a person in a monkey costume walking through the room because they are so preoccupied with everything else they're doing in that moment. This is an example of us being non-mindful because our brain cannot process everything that goes on at every moment. Instead, it chooses to attend to specific things that will be important for us to know. This is why the brain reacts to movement more readily than it does to things that are standing still. It is an instinctual survival method for us to be able to attend to important parts of our environment so our fight/flight/freeze response can activate. If we take a moment relax ourselves and open our eyes, we often become very aware of things that we may not have been aware of before. The process mentioned above of ignoring certain things so that we can focus on more important parts of our lives is sometimes referred to as habituation. This is not to say that habituation is anti-mindful or the opposite of being mindful, in fact this is a natural process our brain completes to allow us to be more effective in our day. Without habituation our brain would become overwhelmed with information and would ultimately be unable to act, making life extremely difficult, or making us blind as a Tiger Beetle on the hunt.

Despite this, taking a moment to expand our awareness seems to have a relaxing and calming effect on the body. Doing mindful exercises gives us a chance to be more in touch with our environment, with others, and with ourselves. Knowing this, we can be a bit more specific about what mindfulness is. Acceptance and Commitment Therapy discusses mindfulness as being aware of the chatter in our minds that direct us to respond to or act on stimulus in the environment. What ACT professes is that taking the opportunity to let go of the negative things our mind is telling us gives us a chance to accept our natural struggle and suffering to ultimately help us observe ourselves and be more present in the here-and-now. ACT does this with a plethora of mindfulness based techniques, a few of which will be discussed in the How chapter of this book. Mindfulness in Dialectical Behavior Therapy is very well defined and is outlined for clients and patients directly. As such, I would like to present a DBT mindfulness definition as the more complex and specific version of mindfulness. DBT says that mindfulness is made up of "what it is" and "how it's done." According to DBT, mindfulness is observing, describing, and participating. In other words, observing ourselves, our surroundings, and others while using language to accurately describe those situations and trying to be involved in reality, as opposed to imagination, leads to an understanding of mindfulness. How we do this is by being non-judgmental, being one-mindful, and is done in an effective way so as not too cause danger or harm to yourself or others. This definition works very well in helping people understand what mindfulness is at its core. DBT also carries several techniques to help clients to become more mindful of themselves and their world. Some of the skills provided by these two therapeutic modalities will be presented in the final chapter of this book. The last school of thought that I would like to share about mindfulness is that of the philosophical perspective.

I would invite you to be careful not to let your bias or opinions keep you from hearing the information provided by such philosophical beliefs as Buddhism, Zen, and Yoga. Again, if you are not Buddhist or a Zen monk or a Yogi, you don't have to be in order to benefit from mindful exercise. While I will not be discussing these philosophies in detail in this book, you will see their influence on the mindfulness movement that continues to spread across the world. Zen Buddhism is where we start to hear the word consciousness and people being aware of their self in the moment. As I said before, the descriptions above come directly from ancient mindfulness practices. Paying attention to one's consciousness is something to be done purposefully, and we need to direct our consciousness to focus on particular things. For example, mindful eating is a practice where one intentionally and purposefully focuses on what they are eating in the moment. In Zen philosophy, the focus is on the present moment and on the experience of the self in that moment. This can bring some amazing insights when done properly. If done incorrectly though, judgements and suffering can become the focus of one's mindful attention, leading to a plethora of other problems. For a great example of this, look up Henry Van Dyke's short story: "Ripening of the Fruit." Yoga has roots in similar beliefs and trainings, but Yoga has the unique quality of bringing one's awareness of the moment through physical actions. Very generally speaking (as there are many forms and types), Yoga is a health practice, and its benefits are outstanding. Attending to our breath, posture, and movement brings an awareness of self that can be quite powerful. If you'd like to get the idea, try practicing something strenuous like a wall-sit and focus on your breathing coupled with the sensations in your body resulting from such physical strain. Here, a great deal of focus is placed on attention to details about the self, including physical, mental, and spiritual aspects.

As you can see, mindfulness has a great deal of commonalities among different practices. It seems to be the case that a well-rounded definition of mindfulness includes purposeful and intentional focus on the present moment, with attention to the self as it exists there, done in a nonjudgmental way that comes from a genuine experience of your world.

Chapter 19: Stress Management

Stress is known to be one of the most widely recognized reasons for ailment in our general public today, thusly you have to figure out how to deal with your stress. Stress is in charge of the breakdowns seeing someone at work, school, and at home, which at that point lead to health issues. Learn how to limit, lighten, or wipe out stress in your life. It is presently perceived in the business field that stress-related issues are one of the most widely recognized reasons for non-appearance in the workplace.

Significant Corporations are currently perceiving the need to deal with your stress and are executing stress decreases programs in the workplace. Stop and check out what's going on in your life right now.

Deal with your Stress in regular day to day existence. Observe the things that happen each day that directly affect your stress levels. Before we can manage the issues that stress makes in our lives, we have to perceive and comprehend what is happening, see what exists, and after that, build up an arrangement and treat the fundamental causes.

Stress is all over. Regardless of whether you are a worker, a chief, jobless, or an understudy, you experience a wide range of stress in your life. Whatever your calling or status throughout everyday life, you can't flee from stress. In any case, there are approaches to adapt to the stress. Stress management incorporates approaches to manage the day by day weight of life. With the correct disposition, you can carry on with a without stress life in the midst of your stressful condition.

DIFFERENT SOURCES OF STRESS IN YOUR LIFE

The underlying advance in stress management is to know the wellsprings of stress in your life. Albeit a few sources are inescapable, you can make approaches to decrease them. In any case, if the wellspring of your stress is avoidable, attempt to discover approaches to keep away from the stressful circumstance with the source.

Due dates

The standard wellspring of stress from work and school works is complying with the time constraint. Be it a report or a task; it is sufficient to give you stresses. A viable stress management in gathering due dates is to take a shot at the undertaking as right on time as could be expected under the circumstances. When you get the undertaking, attempt to take a shot at it the soonest conceivable time to avert a propensity for continually beating the due date. Along these lines, you can even have additional opportunity to survey your work, coming about to unrivaled reports and papers.

Pointless Responsibilities

Another regular wellspring of stress is the point at which you acknowledge obligations that are beyond what you can tolerate. Successful stress management shows individuals how to state no. By just disapproving of obligations, you lessen the measure of stress in your life. Nobody can say what amount is sufficient. Anytime you believe you can't offer time to an additional duty, saying no is the best alternative.

Learn Healthier Ways to Manage Stress

A few people manage stress by smoking, crying, gorging, or undereating and drinking excessively. Despite the fact that this may happen now and again, consistent utilization of these methodologies will cause you more stress than any other time in recent memory. When you anticipate stress or experience it, attempt different stress management systems. Take a walk, have an exercise custom, write in your diary, or play with your pet. These are healthier approaches to stress management. Utilizing the systems, you calm your stress without hurting your body.

Managing stress proficiently is the way to endure an incredible requests. By learning stress management, you can all the more likely adapt to it. You possibly have two choices with regards to this, it is possible that you stop the stress or the stress will murder you. It is your decision, and you should make the correct one.

HEALTHY LIFESTYLE AND WORKPLACE

Stress can have hindering consequences for an individual's body just as their life. Stress brings down the insusceptible framework, in this way, debilitating the body's guards. The individual turns out to be increasingly vulnerable to numerous conceivably hazardous afflictions.

The impacts of stress shift from individual to individual. One individual may build up a moderately sensible sickness, for example, a gastrointestinal condition, while others may encounter all the more conceivably hazardous illness, for example, hypertension or coronary illness. Contingent upon exactly how much stress an individual is encountering, a few conditions may emerge all the while. This is the reason legitimate stress management ought to be learned and rehearsed consistently.

There are numerous approaches to actualize stress management into one's life. One route is by recalling not to take work home. Regardless of whether you work out of your home, it is critical to isolate office time from individual time. Permitting an adequate measure of time every day to appropriately loosen up and unwind is an extraordinary stress management strategy. Investing quality energy with family, perusing a decent book, or cleaning up are extraordinary approaches to decrease stress.

Exercise is another brilliant stress management strategy. There doesn't need to essentially be any sort of formal exercise program, just fusing strolling, biking or notwithstanding cultivating into your life will do the trick. Also, the more pleasant the exercise, the more viable it will be. Many pick yoga as a strategy for stress management. This is a particularly brilliant decision since yoga isn't just physical; however, it likewise includes the mind and soul all in all. Whenever rehearsed all the time, this can be exceptionally recuperating for the body.

Some of the time, the most valuable strategy for stress management is just keeping stressful occasions from occurring in any case. For instance, a work environment could hold an obligatory reoccurring meeting to enable all representatives to voice their sentiments about how things are going and to give criticism. This avoids stress by empowering everybody to talk about issues that may have been irritating them and potentially resolve the issues.

One more approach to counteract or diminish the measure of stress in the work environment is by guaranteeing that there are sufficient representatives to finish assignments in a sensible timeframe. At the point when laborers are surged and need to comply with almost outlandish time constraints all the time, this puts the representatives under a lot of weight, which could bring about expanded sicknesses. It is significant that businesses cling to this, in such a case that a lot of their workers are out on wiped out leave, there will be next to no profitability.

On the off chance that businesses have positively no decision yet to push their representatives to comply with a significant time constraint, at that point, an appropriate method for giving stress management during this period could be offering paid downtime and rewards to compensate the diligent work. On the off chance that this kind of stress management can't be used, at that point, maybe an elective method for loosening up after such a stressful time can be utilized.

Legitimate and normal stress management should be fused into the lives of everybody, regardless of whether they are a housewife with three kids or a CEO of a noteworthy organization. Stress management isn't significant for a healthy way of life, yet additionally, to improve proficiency at the work environment.

THE EASY STRESS MANAGEMENT TECHNIQUES

These are amazing methods that are anything but difficult to learn, and they don't take a great deal of time or exertion. As soon as you notice you don't have opportunity to tune in to a guided unwinding CD, or take an interest in an exercise program or ponder for 30 minutes every day, at that point, these procedures will give you a brisk method to start to battle the impacts of stress. No reasons, everybody possesses energy for this stuff, so how about we get the chance to work!

Procedures I - Just Breathe!

I have individuals approaching me always for straightforward stress management methods to bring some relief. Let's be honest; we are pushing ahead at a pace today that overrides anything in mankind's history. What's more, if I'm not mistaken, we are not doing so well. Simply read the most recent insights with respect to our health in this nation, and the pattern is stunning. We are accomplishing more with less assets and attempting to fit it all in at a completely rankling pace...something must give! All the most recent data and investigation demonstrates to us that the conventional everyday stress in our lives is in charge of 66% of every one of specialists' visits! People, that is everything from the basic cold to coronary illness and malignant growth, and if stress isn't the essential driver of the issue, it is absolutely a contributing component.

I know from individual encounters the impacts that stress can have on the body and our emotional wellness. By a wide margin, the most significant stress management strategy, I generally show individuals initially includes basic relaxing! I recognize what you are thinking...you are as of now breathing throughout the day.

Genuine; however, the majority of you are doing everything incorrectly!

I will watch my associates while they are composing, seriously centered on some venture. Their breathing is so shallow it's astounding they can even support their life! Not exclusively is their breathing shallow, yet it is additionally, for the most part, finished with the upper chest. This isn't an effective method to inhale, and it loots the collection of valuable oxygen. Presently I don't think about you; however, I'm truly excited oxygen is without still, and since I'm not paying for it, I'm going to take in as much as I can. With regards to breathing, you can spend lavishly and be insatiable!

Legitimate breathing starts in the stomach. The stomach goes about as a cries in the body, and as it grows, it maneuvers air into the lungs. Filling the lungs appropriately will furnish you with astounding outcomes in decreasing stress. All that oxygenated tissue will help each procedure of the body, including your capacity to center, digest sustenance, and loosen up muscles, just to give some examples. And for all intents and purposes, each part of your physical and psychological well-being can be improved with legitimate relaxing.

How about we investigate how we can take an appropriate breadth. Put one hand on your chest and your other hand on your stomach. Presently take in a full and complete breath, filling your lungs with however much air as could be expected. When you have got done with breathing in at that point, breathe out, keeping your hands set up. Take another breath, and this time give close consideration to how your hands move. What you're going for is to have the hand on the stomach move outward from the body first as the lungs load up with air. As more air fills the lungs, then the advantage should move outward from the body as your chest extends. When you breathe out, the hand on the chest should move in before the hand on the stomach, and you ought to breathe out completely and totally.

I would prescribe you take 40 full breaths consistently. Incidentally, don't do this at the same time except if you appreciate feeling faint, I don't need you hyperventilating and going out! I like to pick something to remind myself to relax. Ordinarily, I watch the clock, and that can make me begin to feel stress as solid pressure coming into the body. Thus, every time I wind up checking the time, I interruption to take a full diaphragmatic breath. I additionally utilize this method when the telephone rings, so before I answer, I have taken a full breath and felt a flood of unwinding wash over me. It truly causes me plan for whatever I might confront. This additionally functions admirably for those occasions I feel that outrage going ahead because of the day by day open doors for self-awareness and development my multi-year old girls' dramatization brings into my life.

You can't locate a simpler system that can accomplish such a great deal for controlling stress. Attempt this for yourself for the following week. Make the promise to change this one part of your life, and you will start to see the intensity of straightforward stress management strategies. To a limited extent two of this book, we will investigate the intensity of setting a positive expectation

Procedure II - Shake it, Shake it!

One of the most widely recognized territories of the body where we will, in general, hold stress is the strong framework. Stress can make the muscles actually contract and fix, regularly prompting fits and genuine torment. Most of individuals feel this pressure in the upper back and neck, and they can encounter everything from a mellow consuming sensation to weakening agony. Frequently, this is the antecedent to pressure cerebral pains, and it can truly upset our lives.

The greatest issue with strong strain issues is to get the issue before it shows itself as solid torment or cerebral pains. The most concerning issue with this is it very well may be hard to anticipate when this will happen in light of the fact that the torment appears to simply abruptly show up. Be that as it may, it is conceivable to figure out how to feel the strain sneaking in on the off chance that we simply give more consideration to our bodies. In this way, we should investigate how to actually shake that pressure out!

Alright, stand up, give yourself a lot of room and attempt this examination. Start to tenderly shake your correct hand at the wrist. Attempt to seclude only the wrist as you let the pressure start to shake out. Your fingers ought to be free and floppy. Keep in mind; this is a delicate shaking; you are making an effort not to win a challenge here. Do this for around 15 seconds or somewhere in the vicinity and afterward incorporate the lower arm up to the elbow as you keep on shaking. Once more, attempt to let the strain simply wash away as the arm is truly free and floppy. Proceed with like this for an additional 15 seconds. At that point, incorporate the entire right arm, as far as possible up to the shoulder. Everything in the arm is free and floppy now as you delicately shake away any staying strain. Make an effort not to oppose at all and see exactly how free you can make the muscles in your arm. Do this for an additional 15 seconds and afterward stop.

Presently simply let your arm hang down. Look in a mirror, and you, in the event that you have done this accurately, your correct arm will be recognizable longer than the left! You may likewise see a beating or shivering sensation in your fingertips, and your hand may even feel warm and flushed. This is on the grounds that you have freed yourself of the choking strong strain that was available in the arm, and blood and vitality are presently streaming all the more effectively, enabling the arm to feel progressively loose. You have truly shaken the pressure out of the arm, and in doing this, have stepped toward loosening up your body and dealing with your stress.

You will need to rehash this on the opposite side of the body, so you have balance. You can do this in the legs also, beginning with the foot and lower leg and stirring your way up the leg until it is all shaking. When doing the leg shaking, it is a smart thought to relentless yourself on a divider or seat, so you don't free your equalization. You may need to consider a private spot to shake out the strain, except if you need some weird looks and conceivable undesirable consideration! Obviously, in the event that you do this in a bank on a Friday evening, you are ensured to move ideal to the front of the line!

Alright, since the arms and legs are free, you can move to some delicate shoulder shrugs, neck turns, and some other developments and delicate extending that you like to do to help release the storage compartment muscles. On the off chance that you are composing or stuck at a work station throughout the day, I prescribe doing these exercises about once an hour to keep the pressure under control, and you can do them as frequently as you like consistently. Simply make sure to keep everything delicate, free and loose and clearly stop in the event that you feel any torment or unsteadiness.

Presently you are en route to lessening solid pressure. Allow it to shake, shake, and roll.

Chapter 20: Dealing With Negative Thoughts

Another powerful model which can be used to tackle anxiety and stress is the ACT Method. ACT stands for "Acceptance and Commitment Therapy." The ACT Method embraces mindfulness and views much suffering as coming from the relationship between cognition and language. ACT attempts to teach psychological flexibility

– the ability to increase behavior and thinking which serves our goals, and only challenge or change it if it doesn't.

ACT includes six main principles, which are:

1. Acceptance

2. Cognitive Diffusion – Rather than attempting to get rid of a negative thought, itscontext is changed so its negative power is lessened.

3. Being Present – Developing the ability to be present in the moment without judging.

4. Self as Context – Changing our language to provide a different context for what we think about a situation. For example, changing 'there' to 'here' serves to bring the person into the present moment, lessening the attachment to experiences.

5. Values – Concepts that a person uses to decide which of their actions do not include choices based on avoidance, social compliance or fusion (attaching a particular feeling to a specific experience).

As an example, doing something because a close relative thinks you 'should'.

6. Committed Action – Commitment to concrete goals that match values

The ACT method has several components. Further study should be made into the methodology. There is a website address for further information in the bibliography at the end of this book.

As you can see from the different techniques above, there are many methods of learning to have greater control over anxiety and thoughts. These take practice, but a foundation in Mindfulness and approaching anxiety with an acceptance mindset is a key part of learning these techniques.

Please see the further reading section for more detail about learning this method.

Everyday Mindfulness

Using mindfulness in our day-to-day lives can lead to significant lessening of anxiety. This ensures that our practice isn't only limited to 20 minutes of meditation a day.

Rather, it becomes a way of life. With enough practice it can become automatic and habitual as your current anxiety is now.

However, Mindfulness works best when it is incorporated as a holistic approach. This means you pay attention not only to your emotions and anxiety, but to your entire life. Work on the following areas at the same time as practicing your mindfulness:

1. Exercise.

Exercising is an important way to combat anxiety. Stretching tense muscles, and working out agitation, fear or other 'high energy' emotions through physical activity can dramatically lessen their impact. You might choose to exercise in the gym or go for a run. You may also try exercises in mindfulness while exercising. When you feel anxious or stressed, begin with mindful standing yoga and then plan to take a mindful walk.

2. Diet

Your diet is an important place to practice mindfulness. Pay attention to what you put into your body. Caffeine and excess sugar are unhelpful for anxiety, because of the effects they have on the nervous system. Sugar impacts negatively on anxiety because of the sugar highs and crashes it produces. The body interprets these as signs of panic, which exacerbates anxiety.

In addition, eating mindfully can help enrich the experience of nutrition-rich food. You don't have to eat as slowly as in the grape exercise each time, but taking time to chew carefully as well as pay attention to how different foods impact mood and anxiety can help you make better choices about your diet. When you are preparing your dinner or doing the dishes afterward, take some time to mindfully pay attention to what you are doing.

3. Relationships

Relationships also play an important role in managing anxiety. By using a mindful approach to how you relate to loved ones, you can lessen the impact that anxiety often has. For example, the next time you find yourself feeling anxious about a relationship, you can calm yourself using the breathing into anxiety exercise. Then you can use the 'is it true?' thought process to ask yourself if what you fear has a basis in reality.

4. Sleep

Another area that is extremely important to consider is your sleep habits. Getting the correct amount of restful sleep each night is not always easy when you suffer from anxiety. As mentioned earlier, using the mindful yoga exercise and body scan will help you to tackle challenges such as 'monkey mind.'

Sleep hygiene is an important aspect of ensuring you get adequate and good quality sleep. Going to bed and getting up at the same tome each day, as well as avoiding the temptation to nap during the day, helps to regulate your sleep patterns. This, in combination with mindful exercise and mastery over anxiety-based thoughts, will significantly improve symptoms of anxiety.

Preparing for the Journey Ahead

As you prepare to incorporate mindfulness into your life, it's important to remember to take things at your own pace. Mindfulness can sometimes be intense. You are welcoming thoughts and feelings into your mind that you may have spent a long time trying to avoid. That is why cultivating a gentle mindset of curiosity and non-judgement is so important.

Remember that you are the one who decides how far to go during your practices. If a feeling or sensation becomes overwhelming, then you don't have to force yourself to stay with it. Over time you might find you decide to keep with these feelings for short bursts.

As each challenge arises, you will gain a greater sense of freedom in knowing that you have stayed with difficult emotions and thoughts, even if it's only for a few moments.

The important thing is to not push yourself too hard. Mindfulness is not about forcing our practice or overexposing ourselves to painful sensations before we are ready for them. Remember that you have developed anxiety as a coping mechanism, and it's an ingrained way of thinking and behaving. It takes time to learn new ways of thinking and dealing with our thoughts and emotions.

Commit yourself to daily practice, however, and try to incorporate mindfulness into aspects of your life beyond focused meditation. This way you will learn how to form new habits more quickly. Mindfulness isn't something you can practice once a week and expect to see results. It does take dedication.

At times, you might find your practice drops off, or you feel 'stuck' with blockages. Some people find they fall asleep for example during sitting meditation, or they find there are times when anxiety still seems strong. If this happens, don't lose heart. Remember to treat yourself with compassion. Establishing these practices takes time, and berating yourself only feeds into feelings of low self-worth. Try to encourage the curious and gentle attitude toward yourself that mindfulness promotes. If you have spent years feeling anxious and living with feelings of shame or low self-esteem, this can seem hard at first.

One way to help with this challenge is to think about someone or something you feel compassion and care for. It might be your children, or perhaps a loved pet. Connect with those feelings and then ask yourself if it's possible you could extend those same feelings toward yourself. Try to do this with a sense of curiosity. What would it be like to feel that love, compassion and nurturance for yourself?

Tell your family or loved ones about your new practices if you feel they will be supportive, and encourage them to join you or to learn about how mindfulness can help with anxiety.

If you forget to practice or find you are slipping back into old habits, forgive yourself. Similar to moving your attention back to your thoughts or other sensations when it wanders, remind yourself to practice, and then begin again.

As you practice these techniques consistently, you will notice changes. They have been developed and honed over thousands of years, and have stood the test of time. You can know that you are doing your best for yourself and the people around you. I would encourage you to keep exploring mindfulness. There is much more than is presented here, and there may be exercises you can find that take the benefits of mindfulness to a higher level.

For many, these ideas are coupled with prescription medication that helps the brain to function properly. Medicine cannot be ignores in the conversation, but is not always necessary. Please consult your doctor before making any changes to what you may be doing now to deal with anxiety.

Chapter 21: Tips About Mindfulness Exercises

Mindfulness isn't just something you'd do right away. Of course, if you want it to work

in the right way, you have to plan for it. For this, you can try doing the following:

1. Set aside a time of your day for it. When do you practice mindfulness? Would it

be great to do it early in the morning? What about after coming home from work? It's important to set a regular time for you to do it each day so that you would not forget.

Also, ensure that you do it only during that time, and that you recognize it as a time to meditate. 5 to 20 minutes each day is good.

2. Keep a mindfulness journal. Write how you have practiced for the day, how you

felt, and what you think you should do for the next session. This is a good way of keeping

track of your progress, and seeing how mindfulness could work - and is working - for you.

3. Know the right posture. What you have to do is make sure that you're

comfortable. You could either sit on a chair with your feet firmly planted on the ground, or sit on a mat or medicated cushion. If you can't sit, just lie down - but make sure you

don't fall asleep!

4. Breathe deeply. Make sure you breathe from your belly so as not to breathe

shallowly from the chest.

Once you've got that covered, you could start meditating mindfully daily. You could

even make use of various exercises each day - to keep the process from being

monotonous - and so you could actually be able to enjoy the exercises instead of feeling like you're just obligated to do them.

Here is a well explained list of the mindfulness exercises:

☐ **Mindful Breathing** You can practice this one for as little or as long as you'd like.

I would start off small and try it for a couple of minutes. As you get more comfortable, begin to increase the amount of time.

It is very easy and the quickest to start. It will only take ten minutes, more or less, according to your needs or the time that you have to spare. As the name suggests, this meditation technique centers on your breathing - the rhythms and sensations that accompany it.

Step #1: Find a quiet space with no distraction and take up a comfortable posture.

You can sit on a chair, or on the floor, or you can even lie down. Allow your spine to be as straight as possible without it being distracting. You can close your eyes or stare into something calming, like a blank wall, but remember that in this

exercise, the focus is on the breath.

Step #2: Now comes the time for awareness. Don't let any thoughts cloud your

mind, just breathe and feel yourself breathing. Do not think of what you 'should' be doing or if you're doing it right. Remember that mindfulness meditation is not about the destination but the journey and that there is no pressure. All you should do is breathe.

As you do this, your mind may start to wander. This is normal and understandable.

Every time you notice your mind starting to wander, gently lead your thoughts back to your breathing.

Step #3: Do this for 10 minutes or so, the time is up to you. Try to keep your breathing even as you meditate and maintain your mood. Free your mind by focusing on the sound of your breath.

Once you are ready, open your eyes slowly. The experience you have doing this

for the first time may vary from that of others, but remember to have an open

mind and accept what happens. All you really need is to be willing to learn and experience.

☐ Mindful Observation- In this exercise, you can either sit or stand up. All you

need to do is pick an object in your current environment and focus only on that object for one to two minutes. Don't do anything but pay attention to the object

you're looking at. Visually inspect every inch of the object and relax into harmony for as long a period as your concentration will allow you to.

☐ Mindful Listening- This exercise is used to help open your ears to listening to

sounds without judgment. A lot of the things we hear every day are influenced in some way by our prior experiences. Start this exercise by picking out a musical

track you've never heard. Then close your eyes and put on a pair of headphones to

block out all outside sound. Once you've begun listening to the track, try not to

get drawn into any judgments of the music itself or the person singing it. Instead, thinking of nothing else, let yourself follow the music.

☐ Mindful Awareness- This exercise is meant to help you become more aware and

find a deeper appreciation for even the simplest, most mundane tasks. To begin

this exercise, think of something that happens, or that you do, on an everyday

basis. Once you've thought of something, go ahead and do it, only, this time, take

a moment to be mindful of where you are, how the thing you're doing benefits you, and how you're feeling in that precise moment.

☐ Mindful Appreciation- Make a list of 5-10 things in your everyday life that normally go unnoticed or unappreciated. What these things are isn't important. It can be either people or objects. Once you've made your list, start to give thanks and show appreciation for them. The objective of this exercise is to start noticing the things that go on in your life, that you normally take for granted, or let go unnoticed. Try to learn more about these things and appreciate how they benefit your life.

☐ Mindful Immersion- The goal of this exercise is to learn how to be content in the given moment, instead of continually getting caught up in wanting and striving for other things. For this exercise, pick one of your normal tasks. Now, instead of doing it as quickly as possible, take the time to appreciate every aspect of the task while you're completing it. Don't think of finishing it. Immerse yourself in each

action of the task. Feel and become the motions needed to complete the task. You want to align yourself mentally, spiritually, and physically so that you are fully in the moment, enjoying each action you're taking.

☐ Mindful Movement - This exercise involves you doing an intentional movement -

like yoga, walking, or stretching. Your intention during this exercise is to focus on

your body and breath, noticing any sensations when moving and any moments when you're still.

☐ Sitting Meditations- These can last for any period of time from only a few

minutes to over an hour. There are countless variations you can practice, but these

types of meditations often involve using your breath as the main focus of the exercise. Some sitting meditations will also include awareness of your bodily sensations - sounds, feelings, and thoughts.

☐ **Body Scans** These exercises move your focus to attention around your body,

showing curiosity in your experiences while also observing every sensation as you gain awareness of it. They will normally range between 3 minutes and an hour. It is almost a guide for you to be more aware of your own body. In this

method, you must forget your desires or your thoughts on how your body should be or feel. Just let things happen and be as they are.

Step #1: You will want to be comfortable. It is best to start this exercise wearing loose, comfortable clothing. Make sure to loosen your belt if you are wearing one

and to take off your shoes. Once you are comfortable, lie down on a mat on the floor or on your bed. Keep your arms by your sides, palms facing up, and legs about half a foot apart. If you find this position difficult, you can place a towel or a pillow below your knees. It may be a good idea, as well, to have a blanket over you, as you may feel chilly after staying still for so long.

Step #2: You can start on your body scan by simply being aware of the weight of

your body. Be aware of how your body lies heavily against the bed or mat.

Breathe in and out. As you breathe, let your body sink lower into the bed or mat.

Step #3: Focus on your breath. Feel the air as it enters your nose and goes into your lungs, and feel your chest and stomach rise and fall with air. Take a few moments to be aware of your breath.

Step #4: When you feel sufficiently calmed and focused, try to move your

awareness down one of your legs - whichever side you feel most comfortable in

- keep this awareness going right down into your big toe and focus there. Feel

your toe. How does the stillness feel? Is it warm or cool? Can you feel the blood rushing in and out of that appendage? Don't get frustrated if you don't happen to feel anything. Just be aware of the lack of feeling.

Step #5: Visualize the air from your breath traveling through your body and into

that toe you are focusing on. Visualize the air traveling down your body as you breathe in then travel back up and out as you exhale.

Step #6: Widen your awareness to other parts of the foot. To your heel, and the

ball of your foot, up toward your ankle, all the while imagining the air traveling in

and down, up and out, through your foot as you breathe. Slowly move your

awareness from your foot, up to your ankles, to your lower leg, and knees, and then into your thighs. Focus your attention for as long as you think is needed, and when you're ready, release and move on.

Step #7: Repeat these steps as you move your focus through different parts of

your body, focusing, feeling, being aware and accepting, then release and move on. Move your focus up from your feet, to your legs, to your thighs, up into your torso, chest, down your arms and up your neck again. Then, you move on to your face, shift your focus slowly through to your jaw, lips, inside your mouth, to your eyes, your temples, your forehead, making sure you are not frowning, then move

on to the top of your head. Remember to take your time and go slowly through your whole body. Be aware of all the feeling and sensations that you feel as you move up through your body.

Step #8: Once you have gone through your whole body, be aware of your

breathing again. Visualize your breath spanning your entire body, through your lungs and into every cell you have. Visualize yourself awash with oxygen from

your breath and feel your cells gather energy. Each breath is a new wave of

nourishment for your body. Be sensitive to the sensations that follow. Keep doing this for several minutes.

Step #9: Forget your goals, forget that you are meditating, and resign yourself

only in feeling your body, in awareness of you as you are. Now resign yourself to acceptance. Feel your body as it is and feel how complete you are just as you are.

Let this feeling of completeness wash over you. Know that you are and always have been complete, that this feeling is not new or alien, just dormant.

Step #10: When you are ready, open your eyes slowly and gently exit the

meditative state. Take in your surroundings and try to bring your mindfulness with you in your daily life.

☐ Guided Meditations - These are meditations that are led by other people. You can

find a ton of these online for free or a nominal charge. They often come in a

variety of easy to play formats. I suggest you should try as many as possible until you find the ones you are most comfortable with. In these meditations, an expert

will normally walk you through a set of mindfulness exercises and will ensure that you reach a deep meditative state.

☐ Guided Imagery- This is a gentle, yet profound exercise that directs and focuses

your imagination in a more positive manner. These can be simple or very complex.

It is often referred to as visualization, although this technique involves all of your senses and emotions. It has a positive effect on mental health and well-being.

Why Opt for Simple Mindfulness Meditation Exercises?

Simple mindfulness meditation exercises remind you that there is no fast-track to

mindfulness. In fact, different exercises can only cheer for you; they won't reward you

with a state of mindfulness without your cooperation. As the discussions featured in

psychology journals imply, they can only help you if you are willing to adopt them as a habit. They are merely tools; they do not hold the keys to mindfulness.

In this regard, the preference for simple mindfulness meditation exercises is best.

Compared to the more challenging group of exercises, they are suggested. Remember,

one of the aims in achieving mindfulness is to not be caught in an overload of frustrations.

Difficult and nearly impossible bouts may be good for mental endurance, but they can

only drain - especially if you're not yet as flexible mentally. Try to stay away from activities that can result in discouragement.

Chapter 22: Accepting Where You Are To Get Where You Want To Be

Acceptance is a big deal when it comes to working with mindfulness principles. Many people who do not accept their trials and tribulations put a bandage over their problems through drugs and alcohol. This is merely a distraction and does nothing to fix the problem in the end. Actually, it can make it worse.

It is through the peaks and valleys of life that we come to know the good times and the bad. Many times we may find ourselves at the bottom of the pit wondering how we will ever climb out. But in order to know the true light of life, we must also know the opposite.

Reacting in unhealthy ways to your current situation that can cause disease and disorder will just perpetuate the downward spiral. However, if we learn to accept our challenges and hardships while working to fix them, we can feel a weight lifted off our shoulders.

How to accept yourself

Take a moment to think about who you are. What have you accomplished and what has been challenging in your life? How has this formed who are you today?

Release your negative thoughts. Acknowledge that they are not going to help you.

Embrace your flaws. We all have them. Let them go- do not let them get to you.

Increase your self-confidence and self-esteem. Take pride in what you excel at and push yourself to try new things, even if you don't always feel like it.

Give your best. When you know you are giving your best, you will feel better about yourself

Find a way to express yourself. Whether you are feeling happy or sad, you can try to find a creative outlet such as dancing, singing, painting, etc. to move those emotions into the material realm.

A few years ago, I lost a job that I really enjoyed. I had moved cities for the job and put a lot on the line to take it. I was pretty upset about losing that job. I felt like I had lost everything, and I did not handle the situation well at all. I turned to my old vice of smoking cigarettes and drinking too much alcohol.

I eventually managed to crawl my out of the situation by accepting what had happened and working to turn my life around. I began to find new yoga studios to teach at, set up workshops in other cities, restarted my online business, began writing professionally for the first time, and picked up other freelance work in my field that I enjoyed. I was able to sustain myself through multiple forms of income doing things I loved!

I would have never known I could do that before if I had not lost that job. This doorway into being self-sufficient would have never been possible. And I may never have had the courage to travel long term as I have for the past year.

In fact, I now realize that I would not be where I am today if these hardships had not have happened. I would have remained working in Midwest America for the rest of my life instead of having the global impact I am today. Looking back, I wouldn't change a thing- and now I know my habitual patterns dealing with stress and bad news and how to make the mindful choice to break them.

Your Brain on Meditation

"Meditation is nothing but a way to learn how to do a thing totally."

-Osho

The practice of meditation helps to build our response to stress. Do your thoughts ever seem to get in your way or hold you back from your potential? Has there ever been a time that you really wanted to do something, but you stopped yourself out of fear? What if you could turn that fear into a peaceful place to respond from?

Meditation focuses the mind differently than our day-to-day life. There are many tools meditation uses to focus the mind and empower the practitioner. The purpose is not necessarily to get rid of these excess thoughts that cause us fear, but rather how we can cope appropriately. The reason it is so effective is that meditation actually affects our brains directly.

How does it work? Through building our grey matter in our brain.

Grey matter is an important part of overall brain function. Research from Harvard has proven that meditation can spur the growth of it. Grey matter is basically the neuronal cells in the brain that governs muscle control, speech, and memory. It comprises 40% of our brains, so higher levels of grey matter correlate to higher levels of intelligence.

The study at Harvard documented people who practiced meditation every day for a period of 8 weeks. According to MRI results before and after, there was recorded growth in the areas of the brain related to stress, empathy, and memory.

Harvard Study: http://news.harvard.edu/gazette/story/2011/01/eight-weeks-to-a-better-brain/

How Meditation Can Help You Break Bad Habits

"If you have smoked since you were sixteen, every time you pick up a cigarette in the day you are also brainwashing yourself. "In this situation, I pick up a cigarette" sends a little ripple down through consciousness that adds to the "take a cigarette" mound. That's why cigarettes are more difficult than almost anything else to give up. Aside from their physical cravings, we create mental cravings because the habit is very repetitive. The habit of smoking puts itself into every situation. The triggers to that situation are so many that many smokers still sometimes want to smoke even years after they have stopped because the mound is still there." Habits that impact us in a negative way can prevent us from reaching our goals and our true potential- whether it's being happy or starting our dream business. If we continually reinforce negative self-talk, eating habits, or whatever your dilemma may be, we will be stuck in a perpetual cycle.

Many times bad habits start as a coping mechanism. We may continually choose to binge watch television instead of going to the gym when we have a bad day. Other times, we have a biological response compelling us to smoke, drink or use drugs to make us feel better. In the end, it is doing nothing to further ourselves.

A common bad habit of many people in Western culture today is cell phone addiction. Next time you're out to dinner, take a look at how many people have their faces to their cell phones at any given moment. These people on their phones may think they are furthering their connection to others through checking their social media or email, but the truth is they are ignoring the people they are with and missing out on a real human connection in the moment. Which do you think actually provides us with a real sense of connection?

Eliminating bad habits is difficult because we think they benefit us in some way.

This means we must REPLACE our bad habits with GOOD ones!

Instead of saying, "I am going to quit smoking," tell yourself that you will start eating more vegetables in its place! Gnawing on carrots and celery is a great way to ease cravings for the oral fixation that is often related to smoking.

Another important factor is reducing and eliminating bad habit triggers. One of these, of course, is stress. The other may be your environment. It could be something like choosing not to go the bar you regularly attend to drink and smoke, or you may need to completely leave your situation... and travel!

However, when it comes to smoking or food habits, it is best to throw that junk away! The saying goes, out of sight, out of mind. If you don't see them or even have them readily available, it will be that much harder to get them. You would have to really make that effort of breaking your promise to yourself.

Team Up With a Friend

When it comes to breaking habits and starting a mindfulness practice, why do it alone? You could team up with a friend as an accountability buddy. Together, you can put a plan in place to break your bad habit, start your new one, and incorporate mindfulness meditation techniques into your life.

You can start with simple phone calls, schedule meditation dates together, and be there in general for support when one another may need it. This way if you ever feel the urge to fall back into old ways, you have someone who can help you. You don't have to go through it alone!

You are the average of the 5 people you surround yourself with.

Ever heard this one before? It's true, think about it. If you are hanging out with negative people who only eat fast food and get drunk all the time, chances are you will be living that same lifestyle. You don't have to give up your friends, but you should evaluate who you spend your time with, especially if they are influencing you negatively.

Finding new friends can be a powerfully positive experience. If you're not sure where to start, look online for events in what interests you through your social network or Meetup.com.

Exercises to Create a Mindful Lifestyle

"Yoga allows you to find an inner peace that is not ruffled and riled by the endless stresses and struggles of life."

Yoga

There are many different styles of hatha yoga to choose from. It may take some experimentation to discover which one is best for you. You may even need to choose to do one or the other depending on the time of day.

One of the reasons yoga is so effective is that it is a physical exercise practice that cultivates mindfulness. Some people who may not be drawn to exercise normally discover they enjoy yoga because it makes them feel good afterward and their ability to cope with daily life's stresses improves.

Vinyasa Yoga

Vinyasa yoga, also commonly referred to as flow yoga, is the practice of linking movement to breath. It is often a more vigorous and challenging style of yoga. Many who are newer to the practice of yoga may be surprised to find it is more difficult than originally thought. If you have an athletic background, this may be a good place to start.

One of the main components of a vinyasa practice is Sun Salutations. They are used in the beginning to warm up the body and activate it energetically. However, they are also often used to link sequences of postures together. However, it can also be as simple as just moving the arms or moving the body from one position to the next with the breath.

The beauty of vinyasa lies in the connection of the breath to the movement of the body. Here are some exercises you can try to understand this connection.

Breathing Up and Down

Our breath is naturally connected to the currents of energy around us. Inhalations represent the upward current through lifting and lengthening while exhalations represent the downward current through grounding and contracting.

To feel this natural current of energy, find a comfortable seat somewhere. Close your eyes and begin to follow your breath. Feel your inhalation filling you up and your exhalation releasing the air out of your lungs. Take a few moments here to settle in.

When you are ready, on an inhalation, reach your arms up to the sky. Then, as you exhale, press the arms back down to the ground. Notice if your breath matches your movement. Did you reach the top of your movement before the breath? Could you breathe longer to sync it so they match?

Ideally, your movement should match your breath. This means that when you reach the apex of the reach upward, you should be at the end of your inhalation. And the same for the downward movement with the exhalation. When we begin to understand how to sync this up, we create our mind-body connection to be present in the moment.

Yoga Poses for Mindfulness and Meditation

There are basic sitting postures that can help cultivate mindfulness through meditation. The physical practice of yoga was designed to prepare the body for meditation by opening the hips and lengthening the spine. After a period of regular practice, your body may be able to come into these positions naturally, without any preparation.

Easy Pose / Sukhasana

Easy Pose is a simple pose for meditation or beginning a yoga practice. It is a great place to connect with the breath. If your hips or lower back are tight, you will want to have a folded blanket or pillow handy.

Take a seat on the blanket or pillow to elevate the hips. Cross the legs comfortably with one foot in front of the other. Make sure you feel both sitting bones connected to the ground. Stack the shoulders over the hips. Lengthen the spine in the center of the body. Rest the hands on the knees, palms face up or down. Close your eyes and follow your breath.

Thunderbolt Pose / Vajrasana

Thunderbolt Pose is a kneeling position that is similar to the Seiza Position used in Japanese tea ceremonies and zazen meditation techniques. If you have sensitive knees, you may need to modify with props or stick with the Easy Pose for meditation. It is important to be in a place to not cause any harm to the body.

To perform this posture, kneel on the knees and sit the hips on the heels. Stack the shoulders over the hips and lengthen the spine. If the pose is possible but restricted by tightness, place a block underneath your hips for support.

Rest the hands on the thighs and close your eyes. Breathe deeply here and notice if the mind wanders. Bring it back to your body and back to your breath.

Breathwork

"If you want to conquer the anxiety of life, live in the moment, live in the breath."

-Amit Ray

I've given you a brief glimpse of the power of the breath toward the beginning of the book, but there are many ways you can use the breath to live in the moment. Here are a few more breathwork exercises you can try.

Sama Vritti / Equalized Breathing

This breathing technique utilizes breathing that is of even length. This means that the inhalations and exhalations will match one another. Begin by first watching the breath and noticing if there is any discrepancy. Count the breath inside your mind as evenly as you can.

Then, work to make them equal. A 4-count breath is a good starting point. As you inhale, count to 4, and as you exhale, count to 4. Eventually, you can increase to 5 counts and higher as you become more comfortable with this. This exercise will have a positive effect on your mind and body, as you bring fresh oxygen into your bloodstream and increase your lung capacity.

Nadi Shodhana / Alternate Nostril Breath

Nadi Shodhana is an excellent technique for clearing out the nasal passages and evening out the oxygen levels in the brain. To perform this breathing exercise, you will place your index finger and middle finger of your right hand in the space above your brow (third eye area). Inhale through your nose, and as you exhale, close the right nostril with your right thumb. Exhale completely through your left nostril. Then, inhale through your left nostril.

Here, you will begin to alternate. Close your left nostril with the ring and pinky fingers and take the next exhale through the right nostril, releasing the thumb. Then, inhale through the right nostril and close that side with the thumb at the top of the inhalation. Exhale on the left side and continue to repeat. The trick is to remember to inhale through the side that you just exhaled from.

Alternate Nostril Breath is a great way to calm the mind and prepare it for any kind of work, whether it's your office job or writing a paper for school. Energetically, it helps to purify the body, as the Sanskrit name actually translates to "channel purification".

Conclusion

By being aware every day of your thoughts, words, and actions, you will instantly become mindful. The Universe is our friend and it wants to give us what we want because we can get into the habit of saying one thing and doing another which then leaves us in limbo. One of the best ways to shift this is to always choose love, even if it feels humbling because this is how you grow.

Being mindful every day is key and the best way to start is to be aware of each moment. Your positive thoughts will create positive situations in the future so choose the best that you can in each moment. what you speak will reflect back also, so speak your truth but speak it kindly.

The best way to choose love or even be aware of its presence is to meditate. This allows you to connect with the energy of the earth and keeps you grounded. The more you tune in the Universe, the more you'll notice it and this will allow you to really define the love from the ego. The ego is fear based and stops us from doing many things. It stops us from saying sorry, it stops us from learning something from someone else, it even stops us from growing but when we cast this aside, we are left with love and it is that love that allows us to be mindful with others and with our own lives every day.

www.ingramcontent.com/pod-product-compliance
Lightning Source LLC
Chambersburg PA
CBHW072014070526
44583CB00015B/1470